Why do I Suffer?

Why do I Suffer?

Suffering and the Sovereignty of God

John D. Currid

To My Mother:

Mrs Olive "Mac" Currid, an Alzheimer's Sufferer

Copyright © John D. Currid 2004

ISBN 978-1-78191-506-6 – Book
ISBN 978-1-78191-504-2 – ePub
ISBN 978-1-78191-505-9 – Mobi

Published in 2004, reprinted in 2014
by
Christian Focus Publications,
Geanies House, Fearn,
Ross-shire, IV20 1TW,

www.christianfocus.com

Cover design by Alister MacInnes

Printed and bound by
Bell and Bain, Glasgow

Contents

There is a great mystery to human suffering. Questions regarding its existence have plagued humanity since time immemorial. In the ancient Mesopotamian text called 'I Will Praise the Lord of Wisdom', for instance, the author bewails his situation of great affliction, and he seeks answers for it from his deities. He says:

> … I have become like a deaf man.
>   … Once I behaved like a lord,
>   now I have become a slave.
> The fury of my companions destroys me.
> The day is sighing, the night is weeping;
>   The month is silence, mourning is the year.
> I have arrived, I have passed beyond life's span.
> I look about me: evil upon evil!
>   My affliction increases, right I cannot find.
> I implored the god,
>   but he did not turn his countenance;

> I prayed to my goddess,
>   but she did not raise her head …
> Whence come the evil things everywhere?
>> (Pritchard, *Ancient Near Eastern Texts*, 434)

What exactly is suffering? Why do people suffer? How can God allow suffering to exist? Why does there appear to be suffering everywhere? Or, quoting the Mesopotamian author above, 'Whence come the evil things everywhere?' Why do the righteous suffer? Why do the unrighteous prosper?

A common response to these many questions is what I would call *dogmatic wisdom*. When confronted with Job's suffering, his friends—Eliphaz, Bildad, and Zophar—adopted this view of life and its many miseries. It is seen clearly in the statement of Eliphaz in his opening response to Job's afflictions. He says:

> Remember now, who ever perished being innocent?
>   Or where were the upright destroyed?
> According to what I have seen, those who plow iniquity
>   And those who sow trouble harvest it.
> By the breath of God they perish,
>   And by the blast of his anger they come to an end.
>> (Job 4:7-9)

Eliphaz's point is simple and direct: the wicked reap on the earth what they have sown on the earth. Because Job is suffering means that he must have done something to deserve the affliction (cf. Job 8:4; 15:20-26).

In Job 22:1-11, Eliphaz lays specific charges against Job for his many sinful activities. The reason that Job is undergoing suffering, according to this friend, is because of these specific sins that are listed: he oppressed the poor (v. 6) and refused to feed the hungry (v. 7). That is why 'snares surround you, and sudden dread terrifies you, or darkness, so that you cannot see, and an abundance of water covers you' (vv. 10-11).

Such a view of the operation of the universe is quite attractive because it defines everything as either black or white. Evil begets evil, and good begets good. It gives a sense of symmetry to life. There is a perceptible order to things. Dogmatic wisdom also provides a firm basis for ethical judgements: if one has something good happen to him, then he must have done something good to deserve it. If he is the recipient of evil things, on the other hand, he must have earned them by doing something evil himself.

It is true that life often operates that way. In the Scriptures, for example, Israel is directly punished and caused to suffer because of specific sins of idolatry. There is a direct relationship between cause and effect in this instance. The problem is that life does not always work that way. An episode in the life of Jesus may help to explain what is meant. In John 9:1-3, we read:

> And as he passed by, he saw a man blind from birth. And his disciples asked him, saying, 'Rabbi, who sinned, this man or his parents, that he should be born blind?' Jesus answered, 'It was neither that this man sinned, nor his parents; but it was in order that the works of God might be displayed in him.'

As they are passing by the temple and they see a blind man, Jesus' disciples react in much the same way as Job's friends. Here is a man suffering greatly, what was the sin that caused him to be blind? This question reflects a rabbinic principle of the day that says 'There is no death without sin, and there is no suffering without iniquity.'

On one level, dogmatic wisdom is true: there is suffering in the world because of sin. However, it is false on another front, that is, not all suffering is due to specific sins. And that is what Jesus is saying to his disciples. This man is not blind due to a specific sin of his own or his parents, but he is blind so that God might be glorified when Jesus miraculously cures him. Thus, there are other reasons for suffering beyond the mere dogmatic formula of specific sin causes specific suffering.

Dogmatic wisdom denies the unpredictability of God in matters of suffering. So, for instance, there is a great mystery in God regarding why the righteous suffer and the wicked prosper. The fact is that Job's friends were wrong. Many wicked people do not suffer hardly at all here on earth, even though they have done many awful things. And, conversely, many of God's own people suffer harshly in this life. How are we to understand such seeming inequities? Dogmatic wisdom does not provide the right answers. How then are we to come to the right understanding?

To be honest, there is much about suffering that we do not know and we can not comprehend. That may be unsatisfactory, but it is true. We must, however, take heart and comfort in the words of Moses to the people of Israel: 'The secret things belong to the LORD our God, but the things revealed belong to us and to our sons forever, that we may observe all the words of this law' (Deut. 29:29). In this book we will attempt to understand what has been revealed to us by God in his Scriptures regarding the topic of suffering. We will try not to go beyond what the Bible teaches. Beyond it is the mystery of the secret things that belong only to God.

It is also true that when we undergo suffering or the weight of adversity we may not know why. And God is certainly not obligated to tell why we are afflicted. However, the Scriptures provide us with various reasons why people suffer and it gives numerous examples for our teaching. Thus, we are called to gauge our own hearts when we are in the slough of despond. We need to inquire of God and struggle with our situation in order to see why he is dealing with us in this particular way. And, for Christians, we must remember that God is loving and caring toward his people, and he brings all things on them for their good and benefit. A friend of mine, stricken with cancer, once said to me, 'God brought this upon me, he entrusted this to me, because he knew I needed it, that it would be for my own good.' Oh, that all Christians would have that attitude in their walk with Christ, and that God's people would be taught to love Christ that way!

Part I:

God and Calamity

That men may know from the rising to the setting of the sun that there is no one besides Me. I am the LORD, and there is no other; the One forming light and creating darkness; causing well-being and creating calamity; I am the LORD who does all these.

(Isa. 45:6-7)

God, the Creator of all things, doth uphold, direct, dispose, and govern all creatures, actions, and things, from the greatest even to the least, by His most wise and holy providence, according to His infallible foreknowledge, and the free and immutable counsel of His own will, to the praise of the glory of His wisdom, power, justice, goodness, and mercy.

(*Westminster Confession of Faith*, Chapter V:I)

SUFFERING AND THE
SOVEREIGNTY OF GOD

In September, 2001, as almost everyone knows, the twin towers in New York City were destroyed through a ghastly act of terrorism. The cost of the catastrophe was in the billions of dollars and, of greater consequence, thousands of lives were lost. That incident was particularly devastating and tragic to a region of the country already hard hit by economic recession. I remember the television announcers, on a number of separate occasions, asking clergy for some type of explanation of the disaster. Why did that horrible thing happen? Without exception, those interviewed said that God had nothing to do with the incident. It was not His fault or responsibility. It was mere chance, a random happening that brought such devastation at that time and at that place.

Such a view of the operation of the universe is common today. In the best-selling book *When Bad Things Happen to Good People*, Rabbi Kushner explains that perspective with great clarity:

> A drunken driver steers his car over the center line of the highway and collides with the green Chevrolet instead of the red Ford fifty feet farther away. An engine bolt breaks on flight 205 instead of on flight 209, inflicting tragedy on one random group of families rather than another. There is no message in all of that. There is no reason for those particular people to be afflicted rather than others. They happen at random, and randomness is another name for chaos, in those corners of the universe where God's creative light has not yet penetrated. And chaos is evil; not wrong, not malevolent, but evil nonetheless, because by causing tragedies at random, it prevents people from believing in God's goodness. (53)

It is essential that we recognize what Kushner is saying, because so many people (in and out of church) hold to the same view.

In the first place, Kushner argues that bad things happen to people as a result of *chance*. They happen randomly. In other words, the reason that my father contracted cancer and died is simply hit-or-miss. Why my mother fell down and broke her hip was an accident, a mere mishap. This unseen chaotic force in the universe randomly (by 'lottery') killed my father and shattered my mother's hip.

Secondly, according to Kushner, there is no reason, purpose or meaning in affliction. For example, a good friend of mine in high school was killed in a devastating car accident. The entire school was in shock. I vividly remember visiting his house at Christmas, and his presents were unopened under the tree. What a tragedy! Kushner, and many others, would say that 'accident' was a meaningless, insignificant, and purposeless event. Jon Tal Murphree tells of a girl who suffered a similar fate as my friend: 'The child died a victim of casual laws, a victim of circumstance. We have reason to believe that her death was an accident, nothing more' (*A Loving God and a Suffering World*, 46).

Finally, and most significantly, that position states that God has no control over bad things. They stand apart from His will and 'choices.' In other words, chaos is a powerful force that exists and acts independently of God. Another quote from Rabbi Kushner will underscore that point:

> Residual chaos, chance and mischance, things happen for no reason, will continue to be with us, the kind of evil that Milton Steinberg has called "the still unremoved scaffolding of the edifice of God's creativity.' In that case, we will simply have to learn to live with it, sustained and comforted by the knowledge that the earthquake and the accident, like the murder and the robbery, are not the will of God, but represent that aspect of reality which stands independent of His will, and which angers and saddens us. (30)

The number of people who agree with Kushner's conclusions often astounds me. I once asked my freshman religion class whether God had brought AIDS as a form of judgment upon our permissive society. Overwhelmingly, my students' response was outrage that I would even consider God the author or originator of such an evil disease. A typical reaction was, 'My God is a loving God, how could He do anything like that?' Or, 'if God brought AIDS upon our society, then He must be evil.'

Many television preachers subtly teach what Kushner says outright. One Sunday morning I watched a well-known television ministry. There were hundreds of people in the audience. The first few rows of the auditorium were filled with invalids in wheelchairs. The preacher spoke directly to these handicapped persons, 'God wills that you be well mentally, physically, and in every other way. God does not want you to be sick.' At the heart of the preacher's message was the idea or assumption that God does not want people in wheelchairs. The reason a person is in a wheelchair is isolated or independent of God's will for that person's life. It was not God's plan for that person, but by chance it happened anyway. William Barclay puts it like this: 'pain and suffering are never the will of God for his children' (*Testament of Faith*, 44–5).

In the early 1970's, Don McLean wrote a song called *American Pie*. The lyrics of the song centre upon the tragic deaths of Buddy Holly, Richie Valens, and others in a 1950's plane crash. At one point in the ballad, McLean describes God's role in the calamity:

> The three men I admire most,
> The Father, Son, and Holy Ghost,
> They caught the last train to the coast,
> The day the music died.

The point of that stanza is to portray God as having nothing to do with the deaths of Holly and the others. In fact, the verse seems to picture God as helpless to stop the tragedy. There is nothing the Divinity can do and, therefore, He flees the scene.

In the final analysis, what Kushner and so many others believe is that God is limited in His power to control the universe. Chaos wanders unbridled, aimlessly, randomly selecting people to afflict, devastate, and crush. God is impotent to stop the unceasing evil onslaught. It merely 'angers and saddens God even as it angers and saddens us' (Kushner, 30). Yet, in his wrath, hurt, and tears there is not one thing that God can do to halt the endless march of chaos' devastation.

As I have already indicated, such a position on the operation of the universe is popular, in and out of the church. But, is it a true understanding of how the universe runs? Does it accurately and properly portray the roles of God, chaos, and man? For the Christian, there is only one way to gauge the truthfulness of such a view: *what does the Scripture say?* What does the holy, inspired, and inerrant Word of God teach about those things?

The Sovereignty of God

At the very heart and foundation of Scripture is the doctrine of the sovereignty of God. What that means is that God is the Creator of the universe, Lord and Master of all, and His will is the cause of all things. In other words, it is God who is on the throne of the universe, maintaining the creation, directing it, and working all things according to His own will and purpose. The Bible depicts that everything that happens in heaven and on earth occurs because of God's decree, will, and purpose.

Because this doctrine is so central to our study of suffering, let us pursue a greater understanding of it at this point. First of all, sovereignty of God demands that God be viewed as the Creator, Ruler, and Owner of the universe. It is He who sits enthroned forever. Scripture, of course, repeatedly asserts that God stands uplifted on the throne of creation. Note the words of David: 'The earth is the Lord's, and all it contains, the world and those who dwell in it' (Ps. 24:1); 'The LORD has established His throne in the heavens; and His sovereignty rules over all' (Ps. 103:19). Before the entire assembly of Israel, David proclaims the sovereign character of God: 'Blessed art Thou, O LORD God of Israel our father, forever and ever. Thine, O LORD, is the greatness and the power and the glory and the victory and the majesty, indeed everything that is in the heavens and the earth; thine is the dominion, O LORD, and Thou dost exalt Thyself as head over all' (1 Chron. 29:10-11). When Moses tells the Israelites about God's possessions, he simply says, 'Behold, to the LORD your God belong heaven and the highest heavens, the earth and all that is in it' (Deut. 10:14). The reader should also note the following passages: 2 Chronicles 20:6; Nehemiah 9:6; Psalm 22:28; 47:2; 95:3; 145:13; Acts 17:24; and Revelation 19:6.

Sovereignty, however, is more than a mere attribute of God, it is also the *exercise* of His power and superiority. That is to say, sovereignty is not a passive part of God's nature, but it is actively working throughout all of reality. As A.W. Pink explains:

> The sovereignty of God may be defined as the exercise of His supremacy ... God does as He pleases, only as he pleases, always as He pleases ... Divine sovereignty means that God in fact, as well as in name, that He is on the throne of the universe directing all things, working all things 'after the counsel of His own will'.
>
> (Eph. 1:11)

The inspired biblical writers represent God in that manner. The psalmist exclaims for example: 'Whatever the LORD pleases, He does, in heaven and in earth, in the seas and in all deeps' (Ps. 135:6). The words of the Holy Spirit through the prophet Isaiah are particularly telling: 'For I am God, and there is no other; I am God, and there is no one like Me, declaring the end from the beginning and from ancient things which have not been done, saying "My purpose will be established, and I will accomplish all My good pleasure"' (Isa. 46:9-10).

Sovereignty means that God controls and directs all the deeds of men
Solomon observes that 'the mind of man plans his way, but the LORD directs his step' (Prov. 16:9), and 'man's steps are ordained by the LORD, how then can man understand

his way?' (Prov. 20:24). The psalmist agrees, stating, 'The LORD nullifies the counsel of the nations; He frustrates the plans of the peoples. The counsel of the LORD stands forever, the plans of His heart from generation to generation' (Ps. 33:10-11). Observe, especially, the words of the Book of Daniel: 'For His dominion is an everlasting dominion, and His kingdom endures from generation to generation. And all the inhabitants of the earth are accounted as nothing, but He does according to His will in the host of heaven and among the inhabitants of earth; and no one can ward off His hand or say to Him, "What hast Thou done?"' (Dan. 4:34-35).

Sovereignty means that God controls and directs the ways of the animal kingdom

The psalmist describes the relationship in God's own voice: 'For every beast of the forest is Mine, the cattle on a thousand hills. I know every bird of the mountains, and everything that moves in the field is Mine' (Ps. 50:10-11). The Scriptures teach that the animals are totally dependent upon God for their very existence: 'They all wait for Thee, to give them their food in due season. Thou dost open Thy hand, they are satisfied with good. Thou dost hide Thy face, they are dismayed; Thou dost take away their spirit, they expire, and return to the dust' (Ps. 104:27-29). The animals even travel the way God wants them to go, as when they appear before Adam to be named (Gen. 2:19; cf. Gen. 6:20). The LORD, moreover, can make an animal speak when His purpose is being served: 'And the LORD opened the mouth of the donkey, and she said to Balaam, "What have I done to you, that you have struck me these three times?"' (Num. 22:28). Not even the sparrow, one of the smallest of birds, 'will fall to the ground apart from [it being the will of] the Father.' (Matt. 10:29).

Sovereignty means that God controls and directs nature
Scripture strongly emphasizes that such phenomena as the seasons, day and night, and the weather are directly governed by the hand of God. For instance, the psalmist declares 'Thine is the day, Thine is the night; Thou has prepared the light and the sun. Thou has established all the boundaries of the earth; Thou has made summer and winter' (Ps. 74:16-17); 'He sends forth springs in the valleys … He causes the grass to grow for the cattle and vegetation for the labor of man, so that he may bring forth food from the earth … He made the moon for the seasons … Thou dost appoint darkness and it becomes night…' (Ps. 104:10, 14, 19, 20).

That God directs nature is further supported by the fact that the inspired authors never say that 'it is raining' (as if it came on its own), but rather they conclude that God sent the rain. So, Job says about God that 'He gives rain on the earth, and sends water on the fields' (Job 5:10). The words of the prophet Jeremiah should also be noted: 'Let us now fear the LORD our God, who gives rain in its season, both the autumn rain and the spring rain, who keeps for us the appointed weeks of the harvest' (Jer. 5:24). God simply rules nature.

That truth is further supported in Scripture when God causes nature to act unnaturally. So, when Jesus stills the storm on the Sea of Galilee (Luke 8:22-5), or God makes the sun stand still for Joshua (Josh. 10:12-13), or when God causes the shadow to recede for Hezekiah (Isa. 38:8), it is evident that all the elements of nature are in submission to the Holy One of Israel. Nature is God's servant. It does whatsoever He pleases, and can do nothing else.

Sovereignty means that God controls and directs the supernatural
The angels of heaven do God's will and commands: 'Bless the LORD, you His angels, mighty in strength, who perform His word, obeying the voice of His Word!' (Ps. 103:20). Indeed,

'are they not all ministering spirits, sent out to render service for the sake of those who will inherit salvation?' (Heb. 1:14). The word 'angel' (*mal'ak*) even means 'one who carries the message and word of another.' The angels of the heavenly host carry out the work that God has ordered and directed.

It is clear from Scripture, moreover, that God controls the angels and spirits of evil. For example, Psalm 78 tells how God dealt with the rebellious Israelites in the 40 years wilderness wanderings. It says, 'He sent upon them His burning anger, fury, and indignation, and trouble, a band of evil angels' (Ps. 78:49). When God seeks to destroy Ahab, the vile king of Israel, we read the following story (related by the godly prophet Micaiah):

> And Micaiah said, 'Therefore, hear the word of the LORD. I saw the LORD sitting on His throne, and all the host of heaven standing by Him and on His left. And the LORD said, "Who will entice Ahab to go up and fall at Ramoth-gilead?" And one said this while another said that. Then a spirit came forward and stood before the LORD and said, "I will entice him.' And the LORD said to him, "How?" And he said, "I will go out and be a deceiving spirit in the mouth of all his prophets.' Then he said, "You are to entice him and also prevail. Go and do so."'
>
> (1 Kings 22:19-22)

In that scene God is depicted in a sovereign, majestic pose upon His throne. He orders and commands that a deceiving spirit go and entice Ahab. The treacherous, deluding spirit obeys the words of the Lord. It can do no other. (The reader should especially compare Judges 9:23; I Samuel 16:14; 18:10; 19:9; and 2 Thessalonians 2:11).

The only reason that Satan is able to afflict Job is because God permits him to do so (Job 1:12, 2:6). Even the devil is subject to the sovereign hand of God (Matt. 4:10,11; 25:41; Heb. 2:14; I John 3:8).

There is no doctrine so clearly taught in the Bible as the sovereignty of God. God is grandly portrayed as the 'blessed, and only Sovereign, the King of kings, and Lord of lords … to Him be honor and eternal dominion!' (1 Tim. 6:15-16). Berkhof summarizes the doctrine as follows:

> The sovereignty of God is strongly emphasized in Scripture. He is represented as Creator and His will as the cause of all things … He is clothed with absolute authority over the hosts of heaven and the inhabitants of the earth. He upholds all things with His almighty power, and determines the ends which they are destined to serve. He rules as King in the most absolute sense of the word, and all things are dependent on Him and subservient to Him.
>
> (*Systematic Theology*, 76)

The Bible teaches, then, that at this very moment, God sits enthroned over the universe. He is preserving and maintaining His creation by His sovereign hand. Everything in the universe, the whens, the wheres, the hows, and the whys, is determined and directed by the matchless, supreme God.

You may say, that is all well and good, and you agree thus far. But, what about calamity, distress, adversity, and even death? Are those from the hand of God?

Affliction

B.B. Warfield, in the *Hasting's Dictionary of the Bible*, gets to the heart of the matter when he says, 'All things without exception, indeed, are disposed by Him … and if calamity falls upon man it is the Lord that has done it.' In other words, because God is creator and Lord of the universe, nothing can come to pass, whether good or evil, apart from His sovereign will. Such a conclusion is consistent with the doctrinal teaching of the Bible. Note, for example, the words of the prophet Jeremiah when speaking of his own sufferings:

> Who is there who speaks and it comes to pass, Unless the Lord has commanded it? Is it not from the mouth of the Most High That both good and ill [lit. 'evil things'] go forth?
>
> (Lam. 3:37-8)

Job, the great righteous sufferer, draws the same conclusion as Jeremiah. We see in the beginning chapters of Job that that godly man is suddenly, and without warning, plagued with the destruction of all his goods. His animals, servants, and even his children have been consumed by 'the fire of God from heaven' (Job 1:16) and 'a great wind' (Job 1:19). As if his suffering is not complete, Job is physically afflicted, having boils from the sole of his foot to the crown of his head' (Job 2:7). Job's wife immediately confronts him in his tragic state: 'Do you still hold fast your integrity? Curse God and die!' (Job 2:9). Note with great and serious consideration Job's response: 'You speak as one of the foolish women speaks. Shall we indeed accept good from God and not accept adversity?' (Job 2:10).

Both of those biblical figures plainly understand that their sufferings, distresses, and persecutions come from the hand of God. Other passages of Scripture confirm that both good and evil happen because of God's will alone. In Ecclesiastes, Solomon comments on that issue:

> In the day of prosperity be happy, But in the day of adversity consider–God has made the one as well as the other. So that man may not discover   anything that will be after him.
>
> (Eccles. 7:14)

Sovereignty or Chance?

The Bible flatly contradicts the view of many today that adversity occurs randomly. In fact, to claim that suffering happens by chance is to deny the all-pervasive biblical doctrine of the sovereignty of God. Calvin explains further:

> Hence we maintain that by his providence, not heaven and earth and inanimate creatures only, but also the counsels and wills of men are so governed as to move exactly in the course which he has destined. What, then, you will say, does nothing happen fortuitously, nothing contingently? I answer, it was a true saying of Basil the Great, that fortune and chance are heathen terms; the meaning of which ought not to occupy pious minds. For if all success is blessing from God, and calamity and adversity are his curse, there is no place left in human affairs for fortune and chance.
>
> (*Institutes I*, xvii, I., 179)

Frankly, those who contend that God has no control or governance of adversity proclaim an impotent God. He might as well be Santa Claus or the Tooth Fairy who can shower us with blessings and gifts, but who flees at the first sign of trouble. C.H. Spurgeon explains it in a powerful way:

> Men will allow God to be everywhere except on His throne. They will allow Him to be in His workshop to fashion worlds and make stars. They will allow Him to be in His almonry to dispense His alms and bestow His bounties. They will allow Him to sustain the earth and bear up the pillars thereof, or light the lamps of heaven, or rule the waves of the ever-moving ocean; but when God ascends His throne, His creatures then gnash their teeth. And we proclaim an enthroned God, and His right to do as He wills with His own, to dispose of His creatures as He thinks well, without consulting them in the matter; then it is that men turn a deaf ear to us, for God on His throne is not

the God they love. But it is God upon the throne that we love to preach. It is God upon His throne whom we trust.

(Sermon on Matthew 20:15)

When Moses complains that he is not eloquent enough to speak to Pharaoh, God responds, 'Who has made man's mouth? Or who makes him dumb or deaf, or seeing or blind? Is it not I, the Lord?' (Exod. 4:11). In that passage we see dumbness, deafness, and blindness, three things that everyone considers adverse to the human condition. Indeed, can anyone claim that a blind person does not undergo hardship? But, from whence do these afflictions come? *They come from the hand of God.* (See, also, Isa. 45:6-7 and Jer. 32:42.)

It must also be recognized that God always uses a secondary agent when inflicting adversity. Thus, when Job undergoes hardship, it is Satan who directly burdens him. In another instance, God causes Ahab to be deceived by sending a spirit of deception upon him. In all such instances, Scripture clearly reveals God as the controlling, directing force (cf. Matthew 4:1, in which Jesus is led by the Spirit to be tempted by Satan). He is sovereign over all of those events.

Consistent with that teaching is that God brings adversity, calamity, and affliction upon His own people as well as on the heathen. The Holy Spirit, speaking through the prophet Amos, describes a situation in which the Lord inflicts His chosen nation Israel. Since that passage is to the point, we will quote it at length:

> "But I gave you cleanness of teeth in all your cities [i.e., lack of food]
>> And lack of bread in all your places,
> Yet you have not returned to Me,'
>> declares the Lord.
> "And furthermore, I withheld the rain from you

While there were still three months until harvest.
Then I would send rain on one city
    And on another city I would not send rain;
One part would be rained on,
    While the part not rained on would dry up.
So two or three cities
    would stagger to another city to drink water,
But would not be satisfied;
    Yet you have not returned to Me,'
declares the Lord.
    'I smote you with scorching wind and mildew;
And the caterpillar was devouring
    Your many gardens and vineyards,
fig tree and olive tree;
    Yet you have not returned to Me,'
declares the Lord.
    'I sent a plague among you
after the manner of Egypt;
    I slew your young men by the sword
along with your captured horses,
    And I made the stench of your camp
rise up in your nostrils;
    Yet you have not returned to Me,'
declares the Lord.
    'I overthrew you
as God overthrew Sodom and Gomorrah,
    And you were like a firebrand
snatched from a blaze;
    Yet you have not returned to Me,'
declares the Lord.

(Amos 4:6-11)

According to that passage, God has brought many ills upon
His people Israel (cf. similar instances in Isaiah 9:13; Jeremiah 5:3; and, Haggai 2:17). Indeed, He afflicted them with
drought (see, as well, Deuteronomy 11:17), scorching wind

and mildew (see Deuteronomy 28:22), and death by the sword (Jer. 11:22). The Scriptures make clear that the sufferings of the godly as well as the ungodly come from the hand of God.

Saint Augustine gets at the heart of the matter when he says, 'Everything which to vain men seems to happen in nature by accident, occurs only by His word, because it happens only at His command' (*Enarrationes in Psalms, 148*).

Dear Christian, has this study been troubling you? Does it contradict many things that you have been taught about God at church and home? Do you cringe at the thought that God controls and directs the afflictions you have in your life? I would not be surprised if you answered yes to any or all of these questions. For the Christian, however, what should matter is not what you feel, or what your family thinks, or what your church teaches, but only what the Scriptures say. I implore you to do more than read this little study, but search and struggle with God's Word.

In reality, a view of the universe in which nothing occurs, good or evil, apart from God's sovereign hand should be *comforting*. That is to say, the realization that nothing happens in your life without God's direction gives divine meaning and purpose to all things. You suffer, you have joy, you cry, you laugh, you live, you die because God wants that for you (See Ecclesiastes 3:1-8). The Apostle Paul assures us of that truth when he says 'that God causes all things to work together for good to those who love God, to those who are called according to His purpose' (Rom. 8:28).

If what has been said thus far is biblical truth, then we are left with some difficult questions. First, why does God desire anyone to suffer? Secondly, why in particular, do believers, the very people of God, undergo adversity and trials? And, why do the same disasters, calamities, and afflictions happen to the believer as to the unbeliever? Finally, and most importantly, what does all this business have to say about the character of God? The remainder of this book will attempt to answer those questions based upon the teaching of God's Word.

2

SUFFERING AND THE CHARACTER OF GOD

The doctrine of the sovereignty of God teaches that everything that occurs in heaven or on earth, from the greatest to the least, unfolds according to the purpose and plan of God. That is to say, whatsoever comes to pass—God has ordained it. History is his-story, and it belongs to no other. There are simply no surprises for him because he established the story from all eternity (Eph. 1:4; Matt. 25:34). The fact of that doctrine, however, leaves us with some difficult questions to answer. First, if God is sovereign, how can there be sin, depravity, and suffering in the world? How could a providential, holy, loving God permit and direct such monstrous things in the universe? Is God the author of sin? Does the sovereignty of God deny mankind's responsibility? Is man a mere robot? These and other critical questions will be dealt with in this chapter. And we need to be very careful in our examination because we are analysing the very character of God as portrayed in Scripture.

And that leads to the most important issue of all: does the doctrine of the sovereignty of God impugn or cast doubt on the character of God?

Theodicy

Theodicy is the attempt to understand the nature and actions of God in the face of evil and suffering. The first question of theodicy that we want to consider is the seeming disparity that exists between the doctrine of the sovereignty of God and the existence of evil, calamity, and ruin. This is surely not a question that is new in our day, but the Scriptures repeatedly and directly deal with the issue. In Ecclesiastes, Solomon tells us that 'there is nothing new under the sun' (1:9), and it is in that book where we will face head-on the issue as stated.

In Ecclesiastes 3:16–4:16, Solomon raises the question, does the human situation truly fit with the idea of the sovereignty of God? In this section, he advances six arguments that might negate the thesis that God has an all-embracing plan involving every event, person, and thing under heaven. The first argument occurs in chapter 3:16-17. He says,

> Furthermore, I have seen under the sun that in the place of justice there is wickedness, and in the place of righteousness there is wickedness. I said to myself, 'God will judge both the righteous man and the wicked man,' for a time for every matter and for every deed is there.

To the point, Solomon questions that if God is in control, then why is there wickedness where justice should be found? Consider the American justice system, in which, for example, people convicted of first degree murder are on parole in five to ten years. Criminals are let off scot-free due to some technicality. Judges are often corrupt. If God is a God of justice and he is in control, how can those things exist?

The second argument appears in chapter 3:18-21, and it reads:

> I said to myself concerning the sons of men, 'God has surely tested them in order for them to see that they are but beasts.' For the fate of the sons of men and the fate of beasts is the same. As one dies so dies the other; indeed, they all have the same breath and there is no advantage for man over beast, for all is vanity. All go to the same place. All came from the dust and all return to the dust. Who knows that the breath of man ascends upward and the breath of the beast descends downward to the earth?

The author contends that if God is in control of everything, it seems unfair that mankind dies just like the animals. Are we really any different than the beasts? We all come from the dust and we all return to it. Who knows if mankind's eternal state will be any different than the animals?

Chapter 4:1-3 provides the third argument. It says:

> Then I looked again at all the acts of oppression which were being done under the sun. And behold I saw the tears of the oppressed and that they had no one to comfort them; and on the side of their oppressors was power, but they had no one to comfort them. So I congratulated the dead who are already dead more than the living who are still living. But better off than both of them is the one who has never existed, who has never seen the evil activity that is done under the sun.

If God is sovereign, why is there such oppression and tears on the earth? This is similar to questions that are often posed today, such as, if God is in control, why are there so many abortions? Why is there starvation in Ethiopia? Droughts in Sudan? How could a providential God allow such things to exist?

The next indictment appears in chapter 4:4-6. The author comments:

> And I have seen that every labor and every skill which is done is the result of rivalry between a man and his neighbor. This too is vanity and striving after wind. The fool folds his hands and consumes his own flesh. One hand full of rest is better than two fists full of labor and striving after wind.

Solomon has observed that some people work diligently and by every right and good work they acquire skill. Yet, for all this effort they are envied by their neighbor, and their comrades bear grudges against them. How could God decree such jealousies? If he is in control, why is there such selfishness, greed, and inhumanity? On the other hand, there are the sluggards who refuse to work and love their own ease. They put themselves in desperate circumstances. Yet, it appears that the fools gain more than the ones who work hard. Where is the equity? Where is the continuity between work and reward, between right living and justice? How can these things be common if God is running the universe?

The fifth argument is made in chapter 4:7-12. It says:

> Then I looked again at vanity under the sun. There was a certain man without a dependent, having neither a son nor a brother, yet there was no end to all his labor. Indeed, his eyes were not satisfied with riches and he never asked, 'And for whom am I laboring and depriving myself of pleasure?' This too is vanity and it is a grievous task. Two are better than one because they have a good return for their labor. For if either of them falls, the one will lift up his companion. But woe to the one who falls

when there is not another to lift him up. Furthermore, if two lie down together they keep warm, but how can one be warm alone? And if one can overpower him who is alone, two can resist him. A cord of three strands is not quickly torn apart.

Why is there loneliness? Often we see situations like verse 8, in which a person has no family and no one to share in the fruits of his labour. There are many who have no companions, partners, or friends—they are lonely. There are many people today who deal with this very issue. How could God in his providence decree that I have no Christian friends? Could it be his will that I do not marry? What about not having children? Isn't it true that two are better than one (v. 9)?

The final charge comes in chapter 4:13-16. The author comments:

A poor, yet wise lad is better than an old and foolish king, who no longer knows how to receive instruction. For he has come out of prison to become king, even though he was born poor in his kingdom. I have seen all the living under the sun throng to the side of the second lad who replaces him. There is no end to all the people, to all who were before them, and even the ones who will come later will not be happy with him, for this too is vanity and striving after wind.

Solomon here recognizes the fleeting and temporary popularity that is accorded to people. Some people desire to be rich, others famous, and others powerful. He claims that these are all self-defeating wants and desires. In fact, even a poor man in prison could rise to be king in place of Solomon. How can the plan of God encompass the likes of that?

We have all heard the saying, 'If God is a loving God, how could he allow such things to exist?' This question truly brings to the fore the issue of the character of God and, in particular, his sovereignty, because these difficulties do exist. And, here, three thousand years ago, Solomon asks questions that are so commonly asked of God's sovereignty today. Indeed, 'there is nothing new under the sun'!

In chapter 5:1-7, Solomon acknowledges that there are indeed obstacles, in our humanity and our situation, which may lead one not to believe in the providence of God. Would not the death of one's child cause a person easily to question whether or not God is in control of all things? We are called to understand that response and to have compassion on people undergoing such hardship. However, we must also realize that we are merely human and finite in our knowledge and understanding. In verse 2, Solomon says, 'For God is in heaven and you are on the earth…' We should not be seduced by human arguments, but rather stand on the proclamation of God that he is actively in charge of all things!

In other words, we should not be swayed by the six arguments and then be led to adopt an irreligious stance on life. Rather we should 'go to the house of God' with a receptive attitude and listen (v. 1). We ought not to lecture God on how he is to act. Verse 2 indicates that it is a grave matter for a person to question the sovereignty of God. One must not be hasty or impulsive to do it. We must understand our position in relation to God—he rules from heaven above and we do not! He sits enthroned over the universe (Job 38:1-7, 12, 16-18, 31-3; 39:19-20, 26)! And he has told us in his word in no uncertain terms that he is sovereign, and we as his creatures are duty-bound to accept it. There is a time to acknowledge that God is God (cf. Rom. 9:19-21).

In chapter 5:6-7, Solomon provides another answer to the apparent dilemma. He says that the so-called human obstacles of the six arguments ought to be shunned by our lips because they are 'emptiness'. That latter word in Hebrew indicates something that lacks substance and is quickly gone. (cf. its use in Ecclesiastes 1:2 where it is translated 'vanity'.) To the contrary, mankind's task and first order of business is to 'fear God' (v. 7). The Hebrew term for 'fear' means to have 'a reverence for God that leads to obedience.' This means that true piety, a love for God, and an obedience for his word, are the only remedies against the six human arguments that deny and defy the providence of God. In other words, we are called to live by faith and not by sight.

Is God the Author of Sin and Suffering?

Suffering, in its many manifestations, is due to sin. When our first parents sinned, as related in Genesis 3, the effects of that act on all creation were immense. First, humanity itself was greatly affected in all its aspects: (1) Because of their sin, the man and the woman were *alienated from God*. After the sin, they heard God in the garden and they 'hid themselves from the presence of the LORD God among the trees of the garden' (3:8). (2) They were *alienated from each other*. Prior to the sin, they had been naked before one another, a symbol of complete openness and intimacy. Now they covered themselves because they were ashamed. They have fear rather than fellowship. (3) They were *alienated from the Garden of Eden*. In Genesis 3:24, God drove them out of the garden so that they would not continue to have its pleasures, and he placed cherubim and a flaming sword to guard the entrance. (4) They were *alienated from eternal life*. God had told them that they would die if they ate of the fruit of the tree, and the wages of sin is death (Rom. 6:23). (5) Adam and Eve were *alienated from themselves*. The entire *imago dei* ('image of God') was twisted by sin, and so mankind is now corrupt in all aspects of its being. (6) Under

God's commands, Adam was in a period of probation and he was serving as the covenant representative of all mankind. He was the first and the head of God's covenant people. And, thus, what would happen to Adam while on probation, would happen to all people unborn. Because Adam sinned, all people eventually die, they all share in the curses on Adam, and they are all born sinners and at birth held accountable for Adam's original sin. All the descendants of Adam thus bear his nature of fallenness and brokenness.

The fall into sin, however, not only affected mankind, but, in reality, it had great consequences on the entire creation. In Genesis 3:17-18, the very ground is cursed because of mankind's sin: 'Cursed is the ground because of you. In toil you shall eat of it all the days of your life. Both thorns and thistles it shall grow for you.' The ground will now fight mankind's efforts to cultivate it, and the creational mandate (Gen. 1:26-28) will not be easy to fulfil. Because of the fall, creation itself is subject to vanity, futility, and frustration. In Romans 8:20, Paul comments that the whole created order has been 'subjected to futility,' and thereby nature has been severely and negatively affected by the fall. It is what Paul calls 'slavery to corruption' (Rom. 8:21). The universe is in the process of decay and deterioration, and it seems to be running down (Currid, *Hebrew World and Life View*).

To summarize thus far, it is clear that suffering, affliction, and human death are a result of mankind's sin, that is, his disobedience to the revealed word of God. Without sin there would be no suffering. And 'sinfulness thereof proceedeth only from the creature, and not from God, who being most holy and righteous, neither is nor can be the author or approver of sin' (*Westminster Confession of Faith* V:4). But therein lies the rub. For if God is sovereign, that is he controls everything, then is he not responsible for evil, sin, and its resultant suffering? If sovereignty is true then what freedom or responsibility does mankind have? Are they not mere robots?

We must admit and acknowledge at this point that this is a great mystery. To state the question again, how can God be sovereign and yet man be responsible for sin and suffering? These two doctrines appear at odds and even paradoxical. But both doctrines are clearly taught in the Scriptures. For example, in Peter's speech at Pentecost, the disciple says, 'This man [i.e., Jesus], delivered up by the predetermined plan and foreknowledge of God, you nailed to a cross by the hands of godless men and put him to death' (Acts 2:23). The men who crucified Jesus are clearly responsible for that act, yet it unfolded according to the decree of God.

The conflict between God and Pharaoh in the Book of Exodus is a prime example of the issue at hand. Throughout chapters 4–14, the author specifies that God is the one who hardens Pharaoh's heart against the Hebrews (4:21; 7:3; 9:12; 10:1, 20, 27; 14:4, 8). It is clear, however, that God is not making Pharaoh evil or sinful. Pharaoh is evil in and of himself. What God simply does is harden Pharaoh in his nature by giving him over to his sin (Rom. 1:24-26). It is a form of judgement. Is that unfair of God? Absolutely not. As Paul comments, God 'has mercy on whom he desires, and he hardens whom he desires' (Rom. 9:18). Moreover, Pharaoh is responsible for his own condition. It is not as if God is hardening a good person. Pharaoh has sinned wilfully and maliciously. He is not an innocent bystander, but a willing, desiring compatriot of sin and vileness that leads to Hebrew suffering. And that is why numerous references in Exodus 4–14 state that 'Pharaoh hardened his own heart' (7:13, 22; 8:15, 19, 32).

One final example will suffice to clarify the issue. In Acts 4:27-28, the disciples are in the midst of worship after their release from persecution from the authorities. They proclaim, 'For truly in this city there were gathered together against thy holy servant Jesus, whom thou didst anoint, both Herod and Pontius Pilate, along with the Gentiles and the peoples of Israel, to do whatever thy hand and thy purpose predestined to occur.' Again, the people mentioned are responsible for the death of Christ, yet all the events occurred and unfolded according to God's will and plan.

God's sovereignty and mankind's responsibility for sin and suffering are simply and clearly expounded in the Scriptures. They are both true, but how they exist together and at the same time are a mystery. Deuteronomy 29:29 may help us to understand and, perhaps, to accept this mystery. It says, 'The secret things belong to the LORD our God, but the things revealed belong to us and to our sons forever, that we may observe all the words of this law.' What has been revealed to us is the truth of God's sovereignty and mankind's responsibility (his *revealed will*); what has not been disclosed to us is how they exist and work together (his *secret will*).

Permissive Decree

God is not the author or originator of sin and its subsequent suffering. Yet, God has foreordained them because he has foreordained whatsoever comes to pass. And 'sin has come to pass, and God's purpose controls, limits, preserves and governs the universe even in the presence of this fact of sin' (Macleod, *A Faith to Live By*, 40). And, thus, sin and suffering do not exist apart from divine control and purpose. Yet, God does not sin, he does not condone sin, and he does not cause anyone to sin.

God's foreordination in regard to moral evil and sin is *permissive.* 'By his decree God rendered the sinful actions of man infallibly certain without deciding to effectuate them by acting immediately upon and in the finite will ... It should be carefully noted, however, that this permissive decree does not imply a passive permission of something which is not under the control of the divine will' (Berkhof, *Systematic Theology*, 105).

We need also to recognize that God's sovereignty does not eliminate the freedom or contingency of secondary causes. *The Westminster Confession of Faith* says that God's foreordination does not take away the liberty of secondary causes but establishes it (III:I). For instance, it does not eliminate human freedom. It does not destroy our liberty or our responsibility for our actions. Donald Macleod uses the example of Judas to make this point:

> Judas Iscariot betrayed the Lord Jesus Christ; and he betrayed Him by God's determinate counsel and foreknowledge. In other words, God fore-ordained that Judas would betray Jesus. But God also fore-ordained that Judas would betray Him freely, that he would choose to do it and that he would desire to do it. God's fore-ordination does not mean that His whole purpose moved in and forced Judas to this particular act, rather God fore-ordained that, without compulsion or coercion, Judas would freely, volitionally, and with all moral force of his own personality, express himself in betraying the Lord Jesus Christ.
> (*A Faith to Live By*, 42)

Thus, sin and consequent suffering proceed only from the secondary cause, such as mankind and nature; yet everything unfolds according to the plan and will of God.

But why would God allow these things to exist and wreak havoc on the earth? It is simple: God uses secondary causes, be they good or ill, to bring about his purposes and desires on the earth. The situation of Job is a good example. Satan, a secondary agent, is able to persecute Job only because God permits and directs him to do so (Job 1:12). God's purposes in allowing many afflictions to come upon Job are numerous: Job was being taught to lean upon God in times of distress; it serves as a teaching model for the people of God down through the ages; it is for the glory of God; and there are other purposes that could be pointed out as well.

In 1 Kings 22, we read the account of the alliance between Ahab, king of Israel, and Jehoshaphat, king of Judah. Ahab asks Jehoshaphat if he is willing to have his army join Ahab's to fight the Aramaeans. The king of Judah is a godly king who tells Ahab to inquire of the LORD before a decision is made to go to war or not (vv. 2-6). Ahab calls for four hundred prophets, and they tell the two kings that the LORD will give them victory. These, however, are false prophets.

Jehoshephat recognizes that these are false prophets of the LORD. So he asks for a true prophet (v. 7). Micaiah, the son of Imlah, is brought to the palace. He tells the kings what truly lies behind the message of the four hundred prophets. In verse 19, he begins with a picture of God in the absolute sovereignty of his dealings. It is clearly God's design (v. 20) that Ahab should die in the forthcoming battle. And the means that would lead to his destruction is the deception of his mind by the false prophets. The one who is ready to trick Ahab is 'a deceiving spirit' (v. 22). Who is this spirit? Some believe it to be Satan (J. Calvin, M. Henry). And, so, God directs Satan to deceive Ahab by the false prophets. The devil is the secondary agent, and the false prophets are tools in his hand. Others (E. J. Young) understand the spirit merely as a spirit of delusion that comes on the false prophets. No matter, it is evident that God has decreed the death of Ahab and that it will result from a false message having been preached to Ahab.

The death of Christ is the direct consequence of the wicked schemes of Judas Iscariot, Herod, Pontius Pilate, and others (Acts 4:27). They wilfully and maliciously, out of their own devious natures, plotted and sent Jesus to his death. And they, indeed, paid a price for their evil deeds (Acts 1:18-19). Yet, God permitted them to act in those ways because they were bringing about the purposes of God. For these sinful acts were 'to do whatever thy hand and thy purpose predestined to occur' (Acts 4:28).

As we have seen, the sovereignty of God is emphasized in the Bible. Everything that happens in heaven or on earth occurs because of his decretive will. 'God, the Creator of all things, doth uphold, direct, dispose, and govern all creatures, actions, and things, from the greatest even to the least…' (*Westminster Confession of Faith* V:I). Even calamity and suffering come under his purview. But why would God want anyone to suffer and bear affliction? How can this be?

The first thing we must carefully observe is that God foreordains suffering and trials to come on the believer and the unbeliever for different reasons. That is to say, God uses suffering one way in a Christian's life and another way in a non-Christian's life. The next six chapters will define and explain some of the more important ways God uses suffering in the lives of humans. We will begin with a consideration of suffering and the Christian.

Part II:

Why Do Christians Suffer? The Benefits of Affliction

When He killed them [Israel], then they sought Him, and returned and searched diligently for God; and they remembered that God was their rock, and the Most High God their Redeemer.

(Ps. 78:34-5)

The most wise, righteous, and gracious God doth oftentimes leave for a season his own children to manifold temptations, and the corruption of their own hearts, to chastise them for their former sins, or to discover unto them the hidden strength of corruption and deceitfulness of their hearts, that they may be humbled; and to raise them to a more close and constant dependence for their support upon himself, and to make them watchful against all occasions for sin, and for sundry other just and holy ends.

(*Westminster Confession of Faith*, Chapter V:5)

3

SOLACE IN GOD

So far we have seen that the Bible teaches the sovereignty of God. This means that nothing happens on the earth and in heaven apart from the will and decree of Almighty God. That is to say, calamity and blessing, adversity and mercy, affliction and compassion, all arise from the all encompassing plan and purpose of God. Furthermore, we have observed that this doctrine in no way impugns the character of God. He is righteous, holy, just, and pure. In fact, the doctrine of sovereignty rightly perceives God upon the throne of the universe. It understands the full and true nature of God as portrayed in the Scriptures: He majestically rules over everything!

We turn now to some questions we left unanswered at the end of Chapter One. Why does God purpose Christians to suffer? Why does God appoint pain for believers? Sickness? Injury? Persecution? Strife? Hardship? And, moreover, why does God resolve that believers battle the same afflictions as unbelievers?

Prayer

Afflictions quicken the believer to prayer. How many and zealous are the prayers of a believer in times of trial! It is just as David exclaims, 'From the end of the earth I call to Thee, when my heart is faint' (Ps. 61:2). Adversity simply drives the Christian to the throne of grace. Indeed, each of the elect can recount periods of fervent prayer due to suffering. Such episodes are integral to the life of the Christian.

Often such prayer-filled times are due to extreme cases of hardship. Consider, for instance, the example provided by Mr. A. Gracie, a missionary in China at the turn of the century. As with many foreign missionaries at this time (1900), Mr. Gracie's mission group came under attack from Chinese boxers. (The latter was a secret society in China that was fervently anti-foreign; they received their name as 'boxers' because they practised martial arts.) He tells of the chilling incident:

> They searched our persons for silver and valuables, and finding none they took the clothes off my back, leaving me with only my trousers and shoes. After everything was taken, one man noticed Mrs. Gracie's rings, so he jumped up on the cart, with a knife to chop off her finger … then they dragged us out of the carts … The crowds around us kept increasing, calling out, "Kill the foreign devils;" and many of them had every appearance of being able to do the dreadful deed. We fully thought that our end had come, and began praying to God for grace to bear the worst, and, if it might be His will, to so overrule that they might dispatch us without torturing us.
>
> (*Martyred Missionaries of the China Inland Mission*, 220)

The main character, a man named Christian, in John Bunyan's allegory, *The Pilgrim's Progress*, faces similar difficulties. Bunyan relates a scene in which Christian travels through the dreaded Valley of the Shadow of Death:

> About the midst of this valley, I perceived the mouth of Hell
> to be, and it stood also hard by the wayside. Now, thought
> Christian, what shall I do? And ever and anon the flame and
> smoke would come out in such abundance, with sparks and
> hideous noises (things that cared not for Christian's sword, as
> did Apollyon before) that he was forced to put his sword, and
> betake himself to another weapon called All-Prayer: so he cried
> in my hearing, 'O Lord I beseech thee deliver my Soul'
>   (*Pilgrim's Progress*, 97).

Christian responds to his harsh circumstances in the same
way that Mr. Gracie's missions group did—he went to prayer.

A recent drought (1988) in the mid-western United States
wreaked havoc upon food crops. Many farmers were financially devastated by the catastrophe. A common reaction to
the calamity was shown every day on the news: thousands
of farmers and their families joined together in prayer. They
sought God's intervention and assistance to squelch the
drought. In time of need, these people turned to God.

Intense afflictions, as those just mentioned, are beneficial
to the Christian: in earnest, the elect goes into God's presence
seeking His help and consolation. One purpose, then, for the
Christian under trial is it demonstrates our helplessness and
insufficiency to deal with adversity. Believers are simply driven
to lean and depend upon God. As Calvin remarks: '… humbled,
we learn to call upon his power, which alone makes us stand fast
under the weight of afflictions' (*Institutes III*, viii, 2).

The Scriptures themselves teach that an advantage of
intense adversity is a prayer-filled life. For example, we need
only to read many of David's prayers for deliverance in the
Psalms to see the truth of this statement (cf., Ps. 22:11;
25:16-18; 35:15-17; 71:20; 77:2; 86:7; and many others).
From all evidences, God used extreme adversity to prompt

David to pray. Observe, for example, David's response to great tribulation in I Samuel 30:

> Moreover David was greatly distressed because the people spoke of stoning him [David], for all the people were embittered, each one because of his sons and daughters. But David strengthened himself in the LORD his God. Then David said to Abiathar the priest, the son of Ahimelech, 'Please bring me the ephod.' So Abiathar brought the ephod to David. And David inquired of the LORD, saying …
>
> (1 Sam. 30:6-8)

David immediately and without hesitation seeks God's relief in the midst of harsh affliction.

Turning to prayer in times of severe trial is a common reaction of the godly elsewhere in the Old Testament. In the story of Jonah, the prophet tried to flee from the command of God. But God 'appointed a great fish to swallow Jonah' (Jonah 1:17). I cannot imagine a much greater affliction than to be eaten by a fish! In any event, Jonah responded to his adversity by praying: 'And he said, "I called out of my distress to the LORD, and He answered me. I cried for help from the depth of Sheol; Thou didst hear my voice."' (Jonah 2:2). God used extreme hardship to cause Jonah to return to Him in prayer.

Two episodes from the reign of Hezekiah, king of Judah, are particularly exemplary. The first story, recorded in 2 Kings 19, describes the invasion of Judah by the powerful Assyrian army in 701 B.C. During the siege, many of the towns of Judah were destroyed (19:8-11). Basically all that remained untouched was the capital city of Jerusalem, the residence of Hezekiah. At one point in the story we are told that Hezekiah received a message from the Assyrian army. The letter warned that the

Assyrians would soon attack Jerusalem. What a catastrophe awaited the city and the king shut up behind its walls! The Assyrian army, the mightiest and cruelest on earth, was coming to ravage and pillage Jerusalem!

What was Hezekiah to do? Run? Fight? Surrender? No; Hezekiah did as the righteous man does in times of trial. He withdrew to God in prayer. Witness the scene:

> Then Hezekiah took the letter from the hand of the messengers and read it, and he went up to the house of the LORD and spread it out before the LORD. And Hezekiah prayed before the LORD and said, 'O LORD, the God of Israel, who art enthroned above the cherubim, Thou art the God, Thou alone, of all the kingdoms of the earth. Thou hast made heaven and earth. Incline Thine ear, O LORD, and hear; open Thine eyes, O LORD, and see; and listen to the words of Sennacherib, which he has sent to reproach the living God. Truly, O LORD, the kings of Assyria have devastated the nations and their lands and have cast their gods into the fire, for they were not gods but the work of men's hands, wood and stone. So they have destroyed them. And now, O LORD our God, I pray, deliver us from his hand that all the kingdoms of the earth may know that Thou alone, O LORD art God.'
>
> (2 Kings 19:14-19)

In this difficult situation, Hezekiah did not turn to his ministers for advice, nor did he take counsel with his military leaders—rather, he went to God, and Him alone.

In another narrative, the writer of Kings describes Hezekiah's brush with death. He relates that the king was once 'sick to the point of death' (2 Kings 20:1). His illness was so grave that Isaiah the prophet said to him: 'Thus says the LORD, "Set your house in order, for you shall die and not live"' (20:1). Note Hezekiah's reaction to this bad news:

> Then he turned his face to the wall, and prayed to the LORD, saying, "Remember now, O LORD, I beseech Thee, how I have walked before Thee in truth and with a whole heart, and have done what is good in Thy sight." And Hezekiah wept bitterly.
>
> (2 Kings 20:2-3)

Again, Hezekiah responded to adversity by prostrating himself before the throne of grace. He realized he could do nothing about his impending death. As well, he knew that the world and all its wisdom could not benefit him. He, thus, turned to God, the Sovereign Lord of the Universe, and rested and trusted in Him.

Further Old Testament examples of the righteous praying to God because of adversity are profuse. Consider, for example, the cases of Rebekah (Gen. 25:22), Jeremiah (Jer. 21:2), and Israel (Num. 21:4-9; Judg. 20:27).

The New Testament teaches that the Lord Jesus hastened to prayer when afflicted by severe trials. His prayer in the Garden of Gethsamane is an obvious example. In that scene, Jesus knew that He was about to be arrested, tried, and crucified. This adversity drove Him to the throne of mercy:

> And He withdrew from them about a stone's throw, and He knelt down and began to pray, saying, "Father, if Thou art willing, remove this cup from Me; yet not My will, but Thine be done." Now an angel from heaven appeared to Him, strengthening Him. And being in agony He was praying very fervently; and His sweat became like drops of blood, falling down upon the ground.
>
> (Luke 22:41-4)

The reader should also consider Luke 6:12. Jesus is pictured spending all night with God in prayer after a troubling confrontation with the scribes and Pharisees (vv. 1-11).

Moreover, the prayers of the early church resulting from great distress are frequent. We need only ponder the many disciples praying for Peter because of his imprisonment (Acts 12:12), Paul and Silas praying in their chains (Acts 16:25), and Peter's prayer in the raising of Tabitha (Acts 9:40).

Adversity, however, need not be severe to rouse a Christian to prayer. In other words, any type of hardship, no matter how small, may encourage prayer from the believer. I think, for example, how often my wife and I pray for strength when our children misbehave. Or, when I get little sleep and have to go to work, I resort to prayer that God would empower me. Minor sickness can evoke prayer from the believer. In short, the mundane, everyday troubles and anxieties of life can be used by God to bring a believer before His throne. As Calvin rightly said, '…if we shall consider how many dangers at every moment threaten, fear itself will teach that we at no single time may leave off praying' (*Institutes*, xx, 7).

This entire section may be summarized in the words of the Apostle James: 'Is anyone among you suffering? Let him pray' (James 5:13). In plain terms, one reason that God appoints affliction for the believer is to prompt him to prayer. But, as John Newton points out, 'it is a pity it should be so; experience testifies that a long curse of ease and prosperity, without painful changes, has an unhappy tendency to make us cold and formal in secret worship; but troubles rouse our spirits, and constrain us to call upon the Lord in good earnest, when we feel a need of that help which we can only find from him' (*Letters of John Newton*, 173).

The Bible
Afflictions quicken the believer to the Word of God. As prayer is a refuge for the Christian in times of calamity, so is

God's holy Word. When in trouble, the Christian retires to the Scriptures. He reads it, ponders it, and indeed, struggles with it. For example, I had a Christian friend in high school whose mother died a tragic, unforeseen death. I went to see him on the day of the funeral. His father told me he was in his room reading the Bible. He had been wrestling with the Scriptures for three days! Plainly, the Christian withdraws to the Bible in adverse times.

Consider the state of Christianity in the Soviet Union up until recently. The true church in Russia was cruelly persecuted. It was often so severe that believers were imprisoned and even put to death. The Marxist regime desired to eradicate Christianity from the country. In the midst of this dire persecution, only one thing was most precious to the beleaguered Soviet Christian: the Word of God. Who has not heard of stories of the persecuted Soviet Christians hungering for the written Word! Bibles were copied by hand, and smuggled from one congregation to another. The Scriptures are priceless to the Christian who is oppressed and abused.

When hardship occurs, why does the Christian turn to the Bible? There are four main reasons. First, the Christian reads Scripture to find solace and comfort. The Apostle Paul observes, 'For whatever was written in earlier times was written for our instruction, that through perseverance and the comfort of the Scriptures we might have hope' (Rom. 15:4). Bear in mind that Paul was teaching the church at Rome, a congregation which was suffering some persecution (see Romans 5:1-5; 8:35-39). His advice is plain and simple: go to the Scriptures for relief and encouragement.

Second, Scripture restores the downtrodden believer. Affliction frequently demoralizes and discourages the Christian. In some extreme instances of suffering there may appear to be no hope, no haven in the tumultuous storm. God has, however, equipped the Christian with the Bible as a means of restoration and refreshment. Take to heart the words of the psalmist: 'I will never forget Thy precepts, for by them Thou hast revived me' (Ps. 119:93); and, 'This is my comfort in my affliction, that Thy word has revived me' (Ps. 119:50).

Third, scripture strengthens the elect. It equips him to fight temptations and to endure sufferings. In this regard, Jesus is the Christian's model. So, when He was tempted by Satan (Matt. 4:1-11; Luke 4:1-13), Jesus warded off the darts of the devil by the power of God's Word. Jesus answered each of Satan's temptations with a mere 'it is written …' Satan was defeated by the might of the scriptures. The Apostle Paul declares that one of the purposes of the Bible is to fortify the believer: 'And take the helmet of salvation, and the sword of the Spirit, which is the word of God' (Eph. 6:17). In adversity, the Christian hastens to God's Word in order to grasp a weapon of endurance and strength: 'For the word of God is living and active and sharper than any two-edged sword' (Heb. 4:12).

Finally, the Christian turns to the Bible because it teaches him the true nature of his suffering. That is to say, the believer learns and considers God's Word in order to understand his predicament. The Bible is the Word of God and, therefore, it tells the truth about affliction. The psalmist puts it well: 'It is good for me that I was afflicted, so that I may learn Thy statutes' (Ps. 119:71); also, 'The wicked wait for me to destroy me; [therefore] I shall diligently consider Thy testimonies' (Ps. 119:95).

In adversity, the believer does not look to the wisdom of the world. For the wisdom of the world tells him that suffering has no meaning or purpose. Hardship is understood as insignificant. As well, the world says that suffering is merely a result of chance, a hit-or-miss proposition. What comfort lies in the wisdom of the world for the Christian? There is none. The Christian in difficulty, rather, seeks God's wisdom in the Bible. God's Word, indeed, proclaims the truth about suffering.

My point here is clear: God sometimes brings adversity on the Christian so that the Christian would lean and depend upon God's written revelation. Such affliction is beneficial to the believer. John Newton expresses the idea this way:'A child of God cannot but greatly desire a more enlarged and experimental acquaintance with his holy word; and this attainment is greatly promoted by our trials' (*Letters of John Newton*, 173).

Separation from the World

The sufferings of the believer manifest the unsatisfying nature of the present world. The Christian should not seek satisfaction and contentment in the world. The Apostle John says, 'Do not love the world, nor the things in the world. If anyone loves the world, the love of the Father is not in him' (1 John 2:15). Often, however, the Christian takes comfort in the things and ways of the world. God uses adversity to separate the elect from such false contentment. The believer is impelled to turn and lean upon God, who is the only source of true satisfaction and serenity. Thomas Watson explains this purpose of suffering in the following way:

> In prosperity the heart is apt to be divided (Hosea 10:2). The heart cleaves partly to God, and partly to the world ... God draws and the world draws. Now God takes away the world, that the heart may cleave more to Him in sincerity ... when God sets our worldly comforts on fire, then we run to Him, and make our peace with Him.
>
> (*The Divine Comforts*)

This is certainly a scriptural principle. Observe, for example, how David dealt with the persecution described in Psalm 63. He has been driven into the wilderness of Judah, men are seeking to kill him (v. 9), and there are no provisions in the desolate land. David responds, 'O God, Thou art my God; I shall seek Thee earnestly; my soul thirsts for Thee, my flesh yearns for Thee, in a dry and weary land where there is no water' (Ps. 63:1). Through adversity, God separated David from many of the comforts of the world. In other words, He weakened David's attachments to and trust in the world. This, God did for one reason, so that David would turn from a false hope in the things of the world to God. It was for David's benefit that God afflicted him.

God scourged the Israelites during the wilderness wanderings so that they would not become too attached to the world. Note the words of Moses to the people:

> And He humbled you and let you be hungry, and fed you with manna which you did not know, nor did your fathers know, that He might make you understand that man does not live by bread alone, but man lives by everything that proceeds out of the mouth of the LORD.
>
> (Deut. 8:3)

I know a minister who was consumed by making money on the stock-market. He spent many hours each day reading market reports and dealing with a stockbroker. His driving force was to establish security for himself and his family. Thus, when God, in His infinite wisdom, directed the crash of the stock-market in 1987, the minister lost almost everything. Yet, the result in this man's life was that he saw his sin. He realized that he was striving for earthly security, and he had neglected his family, his congregation, and God. And so, by God's grace he humbled himself and repented of his sin. Through adversity, this man came to recognize that only the sovereign God of Israel is the believer's security. Thus, a seemingly disastrous event in the life of the minister was really God's grace at work in his life.

Richard Sibbes summarizes this use of suffering in a marvellous way:

> These depths are left to us, to make us more desirous of heaven; else great men, that are compassed about with earthly comforts, alas, with what zeal they could pray, 'Thy kingdom come,' etc.? No; with Peter they would rather say, 'Master, it is good for us to be here,' Mark ix. 5; and therefore, it is God's usual dealing with great men, to suffer them to fall into spiritual desertions, to smoke them out of the world, whether they will or not.
>
> (*Works of Richard Sibbes*, VI, 162)

The Humbled Believer

Adversity shatters the illusion that we are self-sufficient. It humbles us, and makes us realize our weaknesses. We are made to see our insufficiency in dealing with suffering, sin, and death. Aware of our inadequacies, we turn to and lean upon God, the Rock of Israel. Consider the following story from the book of 2 Chronicles:

> Thus Manasseh misled Judah and the inhabitants of Jerusalem to do more evil than the nations whom the LORD destroyed before the sons of Israel. And the LORD spoke to Manasseh and his people, but they paid no attention. Therefore the LORD brought the commanders of the army of the king of Assyria against them, and they captured Manasseh with hooks, bound him with bronze chains, and took him to Babylon. And when he was in distress, he entreated the LORD his God and humbled himself greatly before the God of his fathers. When

he prayed to Him, He was moved by his entreaty and heard his supplication, and brought him again to Jerusalem to his kingdom. Then Manasseh knew that the LORD was God.

(2 Chron. 33:9-13)

The context of this story is the reign of Manasseh, king of Judah. Scripture tells us that Manasseh's kingship was wicked, and 'he did evil in the sight of the LORD according to the abominations of the nations…' (2 Chron. 33:2). That is to say, the king led the Hebrews into idol worship. He directed the people to carve images, and then bow down to them (33:1-8). The Israelites, thus, abandoned the worship of God. What arrogance and insolence was here displayed by Manasseh and the people of God! They chose to serve the inventions of their own minds and hands, rather than to kneel before the only true God!

Because of the pride of Manasseh and the people, God appointed the powerful Assyrian army to attack Judah. Note that the Chronicler clearly identifies God as the source of the Assyrians 'against them' (33:11). The Assyrian army easily subdued Judah, and they took Manasseh captive. Indeed, the soldiers put 'hooks through his nose, bound him with bronze chains, and took him to Babylon' (33:11).

How did Manasseh respond to his affliction? First, he realized his inability to deal with the situation. The Bible simply says 'he was in distress' (33:12). Impotent and weak, Manasseh knew he could not save himself. Then, he turned to God in prayer, humbling himself 'greatly'. In so doing, Manasseh recognized that it is the LORD who was his only hope of salvation. He understood that God is sovereign Ruler of the universe, and there is no other. As the Chronicler says, 'Then Manasseh knew that the LORD was God' (v. 13). The story ends with God restoring Manasseh to the throne of Judah.

Clearly, God afflicted Manasseh so that the king might be humbled. As Richard Sibbes comments, 'Poverty and affliction take away the fuel that feeds pride.' Through adversity, Manasseh was made to see that he was helpless and powerless in and of himself. Furthermore, by means of affliction, God caused Manasseh to turn to and lean upon Him. The calamity appointed by God was, therefore, beneficial to Manasseh. It brought him back from a dependence upon idols and himself to the true God of Israel. John Calvin explains how this purpose of suffering is used in the life of a Christian:

> First, as we are by nature too inclined to attribute everything to our flesh—unless our feebleness be shown, as it were, to our eyes—we readily esteem our virtue above its due measure. And we do not doubt, whatever happens, that against all difficulties it will remain unbroken and unconquered. Hence we are lifted up into stupid and empty confidence in the flesh; and relying on it, we are then insolently proud against God himself, as if our powers were sufficient without his grace. He can best restrain this arrogance when he proves to us by experience not only the great incapacity but also the frailty under which we labour. Therefore, he afflicts us either with disgrace or poverty, or bereavement, or disease, or other calamities. Utterly unequal to bearing these, in so far as they touch us, we soon succumb to them. Thus humbled, we learn to call upon his power which alone makes us stand fast under the weight of afflictions.
>
> (*Institutes III. 8.2*)

Anne Bronte, in 'He Doeth All Things Well', expresses a similar sentiment using poetry:

> If Thou shouldst bring me back to life,
>   More humble I should be,
> More wise, more strengthened for our strife,
>   More apt to lean on Thee;

Should death be standing at the gate,
  Thus should I keep my vow;
But, Lord, whatever be my fate,
  O let me serve Thee now!

In summary, one of the reasons that God brings adversity on Christians is so they do not cling to the world. How often we rebel against the Lord, refusing to trust and rely upon Him! We simply try to be self-reliant and look to the wisdom of the world. We put our 'trust in princes ... in whom there is no salvation' (Ps. 146:3). God, however, in His unfathomable grace, has 'an excellent means to call us back, and to arouse us from our sluggishness, that our heart may not be too much attached to such foolish inclinations' (John Calvin). In short, God brings His people under the hand of affliction.

By means of adversity, God then restores believers to proper creaturely dependence upon Himself. This is to say that God frequently afflicts Christians that they would again realize their hope, joy, and sufficiency lies in Him alone. God is thus being gracious in adversity, and uprooting the Christian from the world.

Christian, do you suffer this day? Are you undergoing some form of affliction? Are you ill? In pain? It may be that through this trial God is drawing you away from the world, and away from the false security that the world offers. As well, by means of your distress, God may be bringing you to a closer walk with Him. He may be causing you to realize that your only hope and deliverance rests in Him—'Come to Me, all who are weary and heavy laden, and I will give you rest' (Matt. 11:28). Turn to God now in your hardship. Pray to Him, and read the Scriptures.

By no means, however, is this the only reason you might be suffering as a Christian. The next three chapters discuss the further purposes of God in the affliction of believers.

What do you understand by the providence of God? The Almighty and ever-present power of God whereby he still upholds, as it were by his own hand, heaven and earth together with all creatures, and rules in such a way that leaves and grass, rain and drought, fruitful and unfruitful years, food and drink, health and sickness, riches and poverty, and everything else, come to us not by chance but by his fatherly hand.

(The Heidelberg Catechism, Question 27)

Those whom I love, I reprove and discipline; be zealous therefore, and repent.

(Rev. 3:19)

4

Discipline

No one likes to be disciplined. When my wife and I discipline our children (occasionally!), they often do not understand it, and they see it as an unnecessary grievance. It is as if they have a veil over their faces because they can not see that we do such things for their good. I fear that Christians are like that before God. He chastises us for our good but we can not see it; all we focus on is the affliction. It would be better if Christians were like the little girl, who after being punished by her father, climbed into his lap and put her arms around him. She then said, 'Papa, I do love you.' 'Why do you love me, my child?', the father asked. 'Because you try to make me good, papa.'

In the Bible God uses suffering to discipline and correct his people. Believers are objects of God's reproof through affliction. For example, in the Book of Hosea, God rebukes Israel for her apostasy by saying, 'I will go away and return to my place until they acknowledge their guilt and seek my face;

in their affliction they will earnestly seek me' (5:15). Hosea responds by encouraging the people, 'Come let us return to the LORD. For he has torn us, but he will heal us; he has wounded us, but he will bandage us' (6:1). Simply put, God has afflicted Israel because of her idolatrous ways. In this manner, he is calling the nation back to himself—he is correcting the people. God's disciplining of his people takes on various forms and it has a variety of purposes in the Bible. What benefits do God's people receive through the discipline he brings on them? And why does he correct his children?

God loves his people

According to the Scriptures, God is a heavenly father who is good to his people (Ps. 73:1), cares for them, and loves them (Ps. 86:5). This is a wonderful familial metaphor in the Bible, and it is quite common. As the psalmist says, 'Just as a father has compassion on his children, so the LORD has compassion on those who fear him' (Ps. 103:13). Jesus said that we ought to pray to 'Our father who art in heaven' (Matt. 6:9).

Part of a father's love for a son in a family setting is discipline. The author of Proverbs tells us, 'Do not hold back discipline from the child ... [for you will] deliver his soul from Sheol' (Prov. 23:13-14). And, 'A wise son accepts his father's discipline, but a scoffer does not listen to rebuke' (Prov. 13:1). Christians ought to expect correction from their heavenly father. As the writer to the Hebrews says, 'It is for discipline that you endure; God deals with you as sons; for what son is there whom his father does not discipline?' (Heb. 12:7). And God disciplines his people out of love: 'My son, do not reject the discipline of the LORD, or loathe his reproof, for whom the LORD loves he reproves, even as a father, the son in whom he delights' (Prov. 3:11-12). In reference to the forty years of wandering in the wilderness, Moses explained to Israel, 'Thus you are to know in your heart that the LORD your God was disciplining you just as a man disciplines his son' (Deut. 8:5).

When we understand that affliction at times is God's loving discipline of us, then suffering is easier to manage because it is ultimately for our good. Indeed, 'when we are full of this view of God, not a day goes by without detecting something fatherly in him, which we never observed before. Everything about us alters by degrees. Duties grow into privileges; pains soften the heart with a delicious humility, and sorrows are heavenly presences' (F. W. Faber). Remember what Paul proclaims in Romans 8:28, 'And we know that God causes all things to work together for good to those who love God, to those who are called according to his purpose.'

Discipline for Refinement

God disciplines his children in order to refine their character. Suffering is one of the means that he uses for the sanctification of his people. 'We sometimes wonder, with regard to some of God's dealings with the elect, that he should cast them again and again into the crucible of trial. It seems to us though they were already refined gold. But he sees that in them which we do not see, a further fineness which is possible...' (Trench).

The teaching that God builds character in his people by correcting them through suffering is a biblical principle. The psalmist recognizes this truth when he declares:

> For thou has tried us, O God;
>   Thou hast refined us as silver is refined.
> Thou didst bring us into the net;
>   Thou didst lay an oppressive burden
>   upon our loins.
> Thou didst make men ride over our heads;

We went through fire and water;
Yet thou didst bring us out into a place of abundance.
I shall come into thy house with burnt offerings;
I shall pay thee my vows ...

(Ps. 66:10-13)

Several years ago a woman in our congregation became severely ill. On her sick bed, she told the pastor, 'God knew I needed this so that I would cease straying and become more and more like Jesus.' In a letter to a parishioner on a sickbed, Robert Murray McCheyne wrote,

I like to hear from you, and especially when God is revealing Himself to your soul. All his doings are wonderful. It is, indeed, amazing how He makes use of affliction to make us feel His love more ... Does trouble work patience in you? Does it lead you to cling closer to the Lord Jesus – to hide deeper in the rock? Does it make you be still and know that He is God? ... Ah! then you have got the improvement of trouble if it has led you thus.

Discipline as Preparation

A. D. Vail once commented that 'sometimes God tries us when he has in store for us some great undertaking ... It would seem, indeed, to be God's usual method to prepare men for extensive usefulness by the personal discipline of trial.' Moses is a wonderful biblical example of this principle at work. In Exodus 3:1, Moses is pictured as shepherding sheep in the wilderness. And this is no temporary job, but he did this work for forty years. He has gone from a position of royalty in Egypt, the son of Pharaoh's daughter, to being a lowly shepherd. It must have been particularly humbling for Moses because 'all shepherds are detestable to the Egyptians' (Gen. 46:34). He appears to be a tragic figure. He has lost his position of power and authority, his fame, and his wealth. And he is in the lowliest position in a barren and arid land.

But, wait! God's sovereignty is at work here. He is guiding, leading, directing, and moulding events to his own purposes. For here is a poor, sinful shepherd who will one day be the shepherd of Israel. And, in truth, these forty years of demeaning work are training for the task of shepherding the flock of the Lord through these very same harsh and barren lands.

It is like a vaccination for smallpox or some other disease. The inoculation itself is unpleasant, and the side effects are uncomfortable, and the reality is that one is given a minor dose of the disease. However, when confronted with the disease itself, one's immune system is able to fight it because of growing immunity. Thus, one's system is trained and prepared. That is like the Christian life; as Paul says,

> Who shall separate us from the love of Christ? Shall tribulation, or distress, or persecution, or famine, or nakedness, or peril, or sword? Just as it is written, 'For thy sake we are being put to death all day long; we were considered as sheep to be slaughtered.' But in all these things we overwhelmingly conquer through him who loved us'
>
> (Rom. 8:35-37).

Discipline as Instruction

Thomas Brooks once commented, 'God's corrections are instructions, His lashes our lessons, His scourges, our schoolmasters, His chastisements our admonitions! And to note this, the Hebrews and Greeks both do express chastening and teaching by one and the same word, because the latter is the true end of the former.' Indeed, the term for discipline or chastening in Hebrew bears the idea of exercising an educating influence on another (*BDB*, 416). It is often through suffering that we learn something about our own hearts, about God's character, and about the world around us.

In the Book of Ecclesiastes, Solomon asks the question, 'What is good for a man in his lifetime?' (6:12). He then spends considerable time answering that important question. One answer he provides appears in chapter 7, verse 2:

> It is better to go to a house of mourning
>   than to go to a house of feasting,
> because that is the end of every man,
>   and the living takes it to heart.

That is a difficult statement to understand because, of course, most of us believe the exact opposite to be true. But it is the last line that helps us to see Solomon's point: it literally says that 'the living sets it into his heart.' It is in times of affliction and sorrow that the crucial issues of life emerge. At a funeral, the living is confronted with their end—they will die just like the person they are viewing. It is in times of suffering that people are confronted with their own condition of brokenness and futility. Solomon continues:

> Sorrow is better than laughter,
>   for when a face is sad a heart may be happy.
> The heart of the wise is in the house of mourning,
>   while the heart of fools is in the house of pleasure.

(7:3-4)

Again, it is in difficult times that we truly obtain some knowledge of our own hearts. It is sorrow that can bring us to a right recollection, that is, our strength lies in God and it is he who is sovereign.

In affliction, we not only learn about our own hearts, but we learn about God and our relationship to him. William Whately put it this way, 'When you meet with crosses and calamities, say, "Now I see God's justice and God's truth; now I see the hatefulness and hurtfulness of sin; and therefore now I will mourn, not because I am crossed, but because I have deserved this cross, and a worse too." Suffering has the effect of focusing the Christian's mind and heart on what is real and right and good. The psalmist says, 'It is good for me that I was afflicted, that I may learn thy statutes' (Ps. 119:71). Affliction instructs us to obedience. Calvin commented,

> The Lord also has another purpose for afflicting his people: to test their patience and to instruct them to obedience. Not that they can manifest any other obedience to him save what he has given them. But it so pleases him by unmistakable proofs to make manifest and clear the graces which he has conferred upon the saints that these may not lie idle, hidden within. Therefore, by bringing into the open the power and constancy to forbear, with which he has endowed his servants, he is said to test their patience.
> (*Institutes of the Christian Religion* III, VIII, 4)

Suffering can be training in the right way of living and thinking.

Discipline for Restoration

God's discipline of a Christian is ultimately for the purpose of restoration, never for destruction. In the context of great distress, the psalmist proclaims, 'The LORD has disciplined me severely, but he has not given me over to death' (Ps. 118:18). Jeremiah foresees a time when Israel will recognize her sin and the judgement that God has brought on her by admitting, 'Thou hast chastised me, and I was chastised, like an untrained calf; bring me back that I may be restored, for thou art the

LORD my God. For after I turned back, I repented; and after I was instructed, I smote on my thigh; I was ashamed and also humiliated' (Jer. 31:18-19). Indeed, 'a bruised reed he will not break; a smouldering wick he will not snuff out' (Isa. 42:3).

Discipline for restoration can occur on a covenantal, communal level. In Numbers 21, the Hebrews continue their practice of grumbling against God and Moses because of hardships in the wilderness (vv. 4-5). God's patience comes to an end and so he sends serpents among the people for judgement (v. 6). But it is restorative discipline, for the people come to Moses and they say, 'We have sinned, because we have spoken against the LORD and you; intercede with the LORD, that he may remove the serpents from us' (v. 7). And the LORD responds with grace by setting up a bronze serpent for the people's healing. Israel is recovered through correction.

Discipline for restoration also occurs with the individual. Job remarks, 'Behold, how happy is the man whom God reproves, so do not despise the discipline of the Almighty. For he inflicts pain, and gives relief; he wounds, and his hands also heal' (5:17-18). And Paul says, 'For the sorrow that is according to the will of God produces a repentance without regret, leading to salvation; but the sorrow of the world produces death' (2 Cor. 7:10). Paul understood this principle so well that he used it as the basis of his own church discipline. In 1 Corinthians 5, Paul explains that he excommunicated a church member for sexual immorality. He says, 'I have decided to deliver such a one to Satan for the destruction of his flesh, that his spirit may be saved in the day of the Lord Jesus' (v. 5). The Apostle does the same in 1 Timothy 1:20 to Hymenaeus and Alexander 'so that they may be taught not to blaspheme.' For believers, God's discipline is to restore one to the right way, to recover one from sin, and place one on the correct path.

God's Means of Discipline

It is thus clear that God as a heavenly father disciplines his own children for their own good. The next question for us to consider is, what are the means and methods that God uses to correct his own people? A brief study of the opening chapters of the Book of Habakkuk will provide us with the answers to that question.

The book begins with a lament of the prophet. He is bewailing the seeming inactivity of God in the face of evil. He says, 'How long, O LORD, will I call for help, and thou wilt not hear?' (1:2). Why would a sovereign, righteous God allow iniquity to go unpunished? It is evident that the sin spoken of by Habakkuk is the sin of the people of the covenant:

> Why dost thou make me see iniquity,
>   And cause me to look on wickedness?
> Yes, destruction and violence are before me;
>   Strife exists and contention arises.
> Therefore, the law is ignored
>   And justice is never upheld.
>
> (1:3-4a)

Why does God not answer him?

In verses 5-11 God answers Habakkuk in a very striking way. The LORD says, 'Look among the nations! Observe! Be astonished! Wonder! Because I am doing something in your days—you would not believe if you were told' (1:5). Indeed, God's ways are not mankind's ways (Isa. 29:14-16). The wicked people of Judah will be punished, but it will be according to God's timing, judgement, and ways. God's plan is to raise up the Chaldeans to punish Judah (1:6-8).

Because of God's response, Habakkuk utters a second lament (1:12-17). The thrust of it is, how can God punish his own people by using the wicked and evil Chaldeans? The prophet argues, 'Thine eyes are too pure to approve evil, and Thou canst not look on wickedness with favor. Why dost Thou look with favor on those who deal treacherously? Why art Thou silent when the wicked swallow up those more righteous than they?' (1:13). Habakkuk's question is simple and to the point: how can God use a nation that is more wicked than the people of Judah to discipline the people of Judah? This lament calls into question the very character of God—how can a holy God use evil means to accomplish his goal of correcting his people? Is this really just? This is a question of *theodicy*, which is an attempt to understand the actions of God in the face of evil.

God answers Habakkuk's second lament in 2:1-3. In the opening verse, the prophet is in his watchtower waiting for God to speak to him. Calvin says, 'the watchtower is the recesses of the mind, where we withdraw ourselves from the world.' In verse 2 the word of God comes to the prophet, and it is a command that Habakkuk write down his vision on tablets. This act reflects the lasting relevance of the revelation he is about to receive, as well as an act to clarify the vision. The latter purpose of the engraving is evident in the final line of verse 2, which literally reads, 'so that he who runs will be able to read it.' The revelation of the vision is so clear that one who is running in a race could easily read it as he ran by.

The message of the vision is provided in verse 3. God has 'appointed a time' for the Chaldeans to come and discipline Judah. It will not fail, but it will assuredly take place. Who can thwart or delay the word of God? Therefore, Habakkuk questions the use of the Chaldeans to discipline Judah. God responds by saying that is exactly what he is doing. Habakkuk should make no mistake about it, for it is inscribed in stone.

The fact that God uses the Chaldeans to discipline Judah ultimately points to the sovereignty of God. He controls all events that occur in heaven and on earth. Even though Babylon is an ungodly people, God can use them in any way he pleases! And, thus, we see in Amos 4 how God used famine, drought, plagues, mildew, and even death to discipline his people and to restore them to himself.

As Christians, when we undergo suffering we ought to reflect on our own lives. We ought to look deep into our own hearts, and perhaps we may see that God is correcting us and attempting to bring us to the right way of living as one of his children. Suffering tends to focus the mind and the heart on our actions and thoughts. May that be of great benefit to us so that we would become more and more like Jesus Christ.

Remember the word that I said to you, "A slave is not greater than his master". If they persecuted Me, they will also persecute you …

Jesus to His Disciples, John 15:20

What further benefit do we receive from the sacrifice and death of Christ on the cross? That by his power our old self is crucified, put to death, and buried with him, so that the evil passions of our mortal bodies may reign in us no more, but that we may offer ourselves to him as a sacrifice of thanksgiving.

The Heidelberg Catechism, Question 43

5

Conforming to the Image of Christ

We have determined so far that God purposes Christians to suffer for two reasons. First, it is so believers would abandon the false knowledge of the world and hold fast to the truths of God. And, secondly, God causes the elect to suffer in order to develop perseverance in them. Christians become stronger in their faith through adversity. Both of those principles are plainly taught in the Scriptures.

Another reason God prescribes adversity for believers is so they may 'share the sufferings of Christ' (1 Pet. 4:13). That is to say, since Jesus endured a life of agony and peril, his followers will bear similar lives of affliction. As the Master journeyed, so must the servant. The Apostle Peter explained, 'For you [Christians] have been called for this purpose [i.e., to bear up under sorrows], since Christ also suffered for you, leaving you an example for you to follow in His steps…' (1 Pet. 2:21f). Thomas Watson gets at the heart of the matter when he says:

> Would we be a part of Christ's mystical body, and not like Him? His life, as Calvin says, was a series of sufferings 'as a man of sorrows, and acquainted with grief' (Isa. 53:3). He wept, and bled. Was his head crowned with thorns, and do we think to be crowned with roses? It is good to be like Christ, though it be by sufferings.
>
> (*The Divine Comforts*)

Simply put, Christians suffer because Christ suffered.

The remainder of this chapter seeks to understand the sufferings of Christ. Did Jesus suffer? How did He suffer? Why did He suffer? Finally, the chapter will attempt to explain how and why Christians must share in Christ's affliction.

Did Jesus Suffer?

Certain heretical groups (e.g., Docetism) in the early church taught that Jesus did not suffer while on earth. They argued that Jesus' divinity precluded his suffering. Simply stated, since Jesus is God, and God cannot suffer, therefore Jesus cannot suffer. These groups, then concluded that Jesus Christ 'suffered only in appearance', but not in true substance or reality—it was a mere illusion!

According to the Scriptures, however, no teaching could be further from the truth. The Bible informs us that 'when He [Jesus] became man ... he partook of that nature that is remarkably feeble and exposed to suffering' (Jonathan Edwards). In other words, when Jesus, the great God and Saviour, became a man He took on the fullness of human nature. He hungered, grew tired, mourned and thirsted. He thus endured human pain, agony, ridicule, and even death. Consider the words of the writer to the Hebrews:

> Therefore, He [Jesus] had to be like His brethren in all things, that He might become a merciful and faithful high priest in

things pertaining to God, to make propitiation for the sins of the people. For since He Himself was tempted in that which He has suffered, He is able to come to the aid of those who are tempted.

(Heb. 2:17-18)

Note, also, what Paul said to the Church at Philippi:

Have this attitude in yourselves which was also in Christ Jesus, who, although He existed in the form of God, did not regard equality with God a thing to be grasped, but emptied Himself, taking the form of a bond-servant, and being made in the likeness of man. And being found in appearance as a man, He humbled himself by becoming obedient to the point of death, even death on a cross.

(Phil. 2:5-8)

Did Jesus suffer? The Old Testament writers believed that the predicted Messiah would bear great affliction, agony and grief. In fact, they prophesied that he would appear as a 'suffering servant.' Consider the words of Isaiah:

He [the Messiah] was despised and forsaken of men,
  A man of sorrows, and acquainted with grief;
And like one from whom men hide their face,
  He was despised, and we did not esteem Him.

(Isa. 53:3)

In Psalm 22, David also predicted that the coming Redeemer would endure severe affliction. The psalmist pictured the Messiah (in his own words) being tormented and tortured by his enemies. The Messiah laments,

My strength is dried up like a potsherd, And my tongue cleaves to my jaws; And Thou dost lay me in the dust of death. For dogs have surrounded me; A band of evildoers has encompassed me;

> They pierced my hands and my feet. I can count all my bones.
> They look, they stare at me; They divide my garments among
> them, And for my clothing they cast lots.
>
> (Ps. 22:15-18)

Did Jesus suffer? The New Testament teaches that Jesus knew
he must suffer. He even predicted it. Thus, Matthew 16:21
says, 'From that time Jesus Christ began to show His disciples
that He must go to Jerusalem, and *suffer* many things from the
elders and chief priests and scribes, and be killed, and be raised
up on the third day.' He also spoke of it when asked about
the coming of Elijah: 'Elijah already came, and they did not
recognize him, but did to him whatever they wished. So also
the Son of Man is going to *suffer* at their hands' (Matt. 17:12).
Again, Jesus explained that the Kingdom of God would be
established, 'but first He must *suffer* many things and be
rejected by this generation' (Luke 17:25). Jesus' own teachings
thus testified to his life of suffering.

Did Jesus suffer? The events of his life demonstrate that
he did. Reflect, particularly, upon the dreadful scene of Jesus
in the Garden of Gethsemane. There he was about to be
betrayed, tried and crucified. As he awaited the kiss of the
traitor, he went to God in prayer. We read, 'And being in agony
He was praying very fervently; and His sweat became like
drops of blood, falling down upon the ground' (Luke 22:44).
Jesus suffered dearly as he agonized over his impending death.

Did Jesus not suffer on the hill of Calvary? There they
nailed the Son of God to a cross, a most agonizing and cruel
death. There, as he slowly shed his precious blood, the 'rulers
sneered at Him,' and the 'soldiers mocked Him,' and one of
the criminals 'hurled abuse at Him.' There he died a cursed
death, for 'cursed is everyone who hangs on a tree' (Gal. 3:13;

cf., Deut. 21:23). Yet, despite the affliction, Jesus 'endured the cross, despising the shame' (Heb. 12:2).

Did Jesus suffer? Yes, and in a most brutal and toilsome way. The extent of it is summarized by Jonathan Edwards:

> Christ's principal errand in the world was suffering, so agreeably to that errand, he came with such a nature and in such circumstances, as most made way for his suffering; so his whole life was filled up with suffering, he began to suffer in his infancy, but his suffering increased the more he drew near to the close of his life.
>
> (*The Works of Jonathan Edwards II Sermon VI*)

The Nature of Christ's Sufferings

We shall now consider the distinctives of the sufferings of Jesus. What type of affliction did Jesus bear? How severe was his agony? How did Christ respond to adversity? Those and other questions will be answered in this section of the study.

Observe, first of all, that Jesus' sufferings were unto death. His was not a momentary pang. It was not a hardship that soon disappears. No; every moment of agony, peril, and trouble in Christ's life led to a climatic period of suffering, that is, the betrayal and crucifixion. Jesus suffered unto the very point of death, a suffering of extremity. One only needs to consider the crucifixion scene:

> And the people stood by looking on. And even the rulers were sneering at Him … And the soldiers also mocked Him … And one of the criminals who were hanged there was hurling abuse at Him …
>
> (Luke 23:35-39)

Jesus' suffering was also, at least according to human standards, one of disgrace, reproach, and dishonour. The author of the Hebrews explained it this way: 'Therefore Jesus also, that He might sanctify the people through His own blood, suffered outside the gate. Hence, let us go out to Him outside the camp, bearing His reproach' (Heb. 13:12-13). The expression 'outside the gate' or 'outside the camp' is a reference to Old Testament practice. According to Mosaic Law, those people who were defiled, profane, or unclean were consigned to a place 'outside the camp' of Israel. Thus, lepers, people with discharges, and ones who had touched a dead person were sent to live beyond the bounds of the Israelite encampment (see, Leviticus 13:46; Numbers 12:10, 14-15). This was done so that 'they will not defile their camp where I dwell in their midst' (Num. 5:3). As well, the criminal who had sinned grievously against the laws of God was stoned 'outside the camp' (see, Leviticus 24:23; Numbers 15:35). A person who was set or killed outside of Israel's camp was greatly shamed and humiliated. That it is said that Jesus 'suffered outside the gate' similarly signifies his degradation and derision (in the eyes of the world).

A second passage that reveals the mortification of Christ in his suffering and death is Galatians 3:13. The apostle declared that, 'Christ redeemed us from the curse of the Law, having become a curse for us—for it is written, "Cursed is everyone who hangs from a tree."' Paul quoted Deuteronomy 21:22-3 from the Mosaic Law in this description of Christ's death. That law passage claimed that anyone who hangs on a tree (i.e., is crucified) is a criminal and accursed of God. The Hebrew term for 'accursed' (*qalal*) literally means to be debased and degraded. In other words, Jewish law deemed one who died by crucifixion a shameful and contemptible being. Thus, that Jesus died that way is loathsome and deplorable to Torah law.

A third characteristic of the Lord's suffering was its vicarious nature. That is to say, Jesus endured great miseries (even the cross!) not for himself, but for others. He suffered as a substitution for sinners. Jesus was their replacement. The prophet Isaiah had foretold this:

Surely our griefs He himself bore,
  And our sorrows He carried;
Yet we ourselves esteemed Him stricken,
  Smitten of God and afflicted.
But He was pierced through for our transgressions,
  He was crushed for our iniquities;
The chastening for our well-being fell upon Him,
  And by His scourging we are healed.

(Isa. 53:4-5)

The Apostle Peter put it this way: 'He Himself [Jesus] bore our sins in His body on the cross, that we might die to sin and live to righteousness; for by His wounds you were healed' (1 Pet. 2:24).

Implicit to the vicarious work of Christ was the undeserving nature of his sufferings. He was worthy of none of the anguish, pain, and torment of his earthly life. He was sinless, and, therefore, not deserving of death (see Rom. 6:23). He was God and thus not worthy of insult! Yet, Jesus 'our great God and Saviour' humbled himself to be born a man, to live a life of sorrow, and to die a criminal's death.

Fourthly, the Lord suffered with patience in the face of hardship. Never did he utter a complaint. Never did he feel sorry for himself. Never did he strike out against those who abused Him. Peter remarked, 'And while being reviled, He did not revile in return; while suffering, He uttered no threats, but kept entrusting Himself to Him who judges righteously' (1 Pet. 2:23). The prophet Isaiah predicted that long-suffering would be the trademark of the Messiah: 'He was oppressed and He was afflicted, yet He did not open His mouth; like a lamb that is led to slaughter, and like a sheep that is silent before its shearers, so He did not open His mouth' (Isa. 53:7).

Jesus' treatment and attitude in his court trials is worthy of our consideration. Thus, after false witnesses were brought before the Sanhedrin to testify against Jesus, we read: 'And the high priest stood up and said to Him, "Do You make no answer? What is it that these men are testifying against You?" But Jesus kept silent' (Matt. 26:62-63 cf., Mark 14:60-61). Later, Jesus was delivered to the courts of the Romans under the judgment of Pontius Pilate. We observe that Jesus was again charged by the Jewish leaders:

> And while He was being accused by the chief priests and elders, He made no answer. Then Pilate said to Him, 'Do you not hear how many things they testify against You?' And He did not answer Him with regard to even a single charge, so that the governor was quite amazed.
>
> (Matt. 27:12-14)

Finally, Luke reported that Jesus acted similarly when confronted with abuse and ridicule in the courts of Herod (see Luke 23:8-11).

In all those sufferings, Jesus did not retaliate in anger. He did not seek to punish those who abused him. Even on the cross, where he hung in such agony and pain, He did not lash out at his enemies. Rather, he interceded for them: 'Father, forgive them; for they do not know what they are doing' (Luke 23:34a). His circumstances, moreover, never brought a complaint from his lips. Nor did he plead for his life.

Jesus led a life of extreme suffering. In fact, no man has suffered as much. As well, no man could withstand such trials and tribulations. There never was sorrow like unto his sorrow.

The Purpose of Christ's Sufferings
Why did Jesus withstand such torment? Why did he submit to being set 'outside the camp' and to being accursed? Why did he persevere in the midst of such agony and shame?

The principal reason that Jesus endured a life of suffering unto death was because God had decreed it. In other words, Christ had been appointed by God 'before the foundation of the world' (1 Pet. 1:20) to suffer and die upon the cross. Note the words of Peter from his sermon to the Jews on the Day of Pentecost: 'Jesus the Nazarene … this man, delivered up by the predetermined plan and foreknowledge of God, you nailed to a cross by the hands of godless men and put Him to death' (Acts 2:22-3). And consider the prayer of the disciples in Acts 4: 'For truly in this city there were gathered together against Thy holy servant Jesus, whom Thou didst anoint, both Herod and Pontius Pilate, along with the Gentiles and the people of Israel, to do whatever Thy hand and Thy purpose predestined to occur' (Acts 4:27-8). Here again we are told that God predetermined that Jesus Christ would live a life of persecution and have a cruel death. Christ's suffering was simply part of the eternal plan of God.

Jesus knew that he had been chosen and ordained to suffer. Thus, during the Lord's Supper shortly before His death, Jesus said, 'For indeed, the Son of Man is going as it has been determined' (Luke 22:22). The reader should also reflect on these passages: Matthew 16:21; 17:12; Mark 8:31; 9:12; Luke 9:22; 17:25.

Jesus also suffered in order to fulfil the Old Testament messianic prophecies. Indeed, the prophets had predicted a coming Redeemer who would be humble and suffer for his people (see, Psalm 22, Isaiah 53; Zechariah 9:9). Jesus' pain and agony attested to his fulfilling those ancient promises. He was the expected Messiah. Consider Peter's remark to the Jews at the temple: 'But the things which God announced beforehand by the mouth of all the prophets, that His Christ should suffer, He has thus fulfilled' (Acts 3:18). When Paul witnessed in synagogues, he also taught that Jesus' suffering realized Old Testament prophecy: 'And according to Paul's custom, he went to them, and for three Sabbaths reasoned with them from the Scriptures, explaining and giving evidence that the Christ had to suffer and rise again from the dead, and saying, "This Jesus whom I am proclaiming to you is the Christ"' (Acts 17:2-3).

Jesus himself knew his afflictions were in fulfilment of Old Testament prophecy. The post-resurrection scene on the Emmaus road supports this conclusion (Luke 24). There, two disciples were travelling home after the death and burial of Jesus. They simply failed to understand that the Old Testament foretold a suffering Redeemer. (A prominent belief of Judaism during New Testament times was that the promised Messiah would restore the physical nation of Israel. This appears to be the belief of these two disciples—see v. 21.) The risen Jesus appeared to them and said, "'O foolish men and slow of heart to believe in all that the prophets have spoken! Was it not necessary for the Christ to suffer these things and to enter into His glory?" And beginning with Moses and with all the prophets, He explained to them the things concerning Himself in all the Scriptures' (Luke 24:25-27). Jesus simply revealed to the disciples that the task of the Messiah, according to the Old Testament, was to suffer and die.

The sufferings of Jesus were, furthermore, the means by which God ordained the redemption of his people. That is to say, the elect have been restored to a right relationship with God through the precious blood of Jesus Christ. As Peter remarked, 'For Christ also died for sins once for all, the just for the unjust, in order that He might bring us to God, having been put to death in the flesh…' (1 Pet. 3:18); and, 'He Himself bore our sins in His body on the cross, that we might die to sin and live to righteousness' (1 Pet. 2:24).

In connection with the redemption of mankind, the sufferings of Christ also conquered Satan. The writer to the Hebrews commented, 'Since then the children share in flesh and blood, He himself also partook of the same, that through death He might render powerless him who had the power of death, that is, the devil' (Heb. 2:14). It is truly ironic that the agony of Christ was what defeated Satan. Jesus did not claim victory by the sword, as so many had hoped, but by the intense suffering unto death. He was gloriously triumphant through blood, sweat, and tears!

In addition, Jesus also suffered greatly so that He could comfort His people who face adversity. 'For since He Himself was tempted in that which He has suffered, He is able to come to the aid of those who are tempted' (Heb. 2:18). That means that Christ has compassion and grants his mercy to the elect, 'For we do not have a high priest who cannot sympathize with our weakness, but one who has been tempted in all things as we are, yet without sin' (Heb. 4:15). The Lord travelled the hard road that we journey and He did not falter. The Christian may obtain great comfort when undergoing hardship, 'For consider Him who has endured such hostility by sinners against Himself, so that you may not grow weary and lose heart' (Heb. 12:3).

Finally, the sufferings of Christ are an example and a pattern for Christians. All believers undergo many hardships, trials, and afflictions. As Paul said, 'all who desire to live godly in Christ Jesus will be persecuted' (2 Tim. 3:12). We are simply called to 'share the sufferings of Christ'. As such, the Bible instructs us to mirror the attitude and manner of Jesus: 'For you have been called for this purpose [i.e., to bear up under sorrows], since Christ also suffered for you, leaving you an example for you to follow in His steps' (1 Pet. 2:21).

Why Christians Should Follow Christ's Example

In adversity, believers are to conform to the pattern set by Christ because they have been commanded to do so. Thus, Jesus charged His disciples, saying, 'If anyone wishes to come after Me, let him deny himself and take up his cross daily, and follow Me' (Luke 9:23). Christians are to embrace the cross as their way of life. In other words, the sufferings of Christ are the Christians' allotment on earth. Jesus did not offer His followers riches or earthly pleasures. The cost of discipleship is suffering as Christ suffered, possibly even unto death. Bonhoeffer puts it well: 'When Christ calls a man He bids Him come and die.'

Rev. Richard Wurmbrand tells of his preaching the gospel to 1000 people at a university in Romania. He did this at great danger from the Communist authorities who threatened to imprison him and others. He remembers that at the time he received advice from a local pastor (who, by the way, was later martyred):

> You give your body as a sacrifice to God when you give it to all who wish to beat and mock you. Jesus, knowing His crucifixion near, said, 'My time is at hand.' His time was the time of suffering, the charge He had received from His Father, and it was His joy to suffer for the salvation of mankind. *We, too should regard suffering as a charge given us by God.* St. Paul wrote, in the Epistle to the Romans (12:1): 'My brothers, I implore you by God's mercy to offer your very selves to Him: a living sacrifice, dedicated and fit for His acceptance.'
>
> (*Christ in the Communist Prisons*, pp.177–8)

Like Jesus, Christians are simply summoned by God to suffer.

Secondly, when we walk the path that Jesus walked we are strengthened in the midst of our trials. Because we know that our Lord forged the weary way before us and that he travels with us now, our burden is lighter and our journey is easier.

Thus, the New Testament writer encou
the Hebrews in time of great persecutio
who has endured such hostility by sinne
that you may not grow weary and lose h

A modern example is cited by Br
the persecution of missionaries in Shan-
during the Boxer Rebellion of 1900. He shares a letter written
from a missionary to her parents.

> The sufferings and privations we endured cannot be told, and
> I do not want to dwell upon them. The Master suffered, so must
> we follow in His footsteps, at least it is reserved for some to do
> so. May He accept how we bore it for His name's sake. I can truly
> say—even for the little ones of the party—no hatred seemed to
> be felt. Those of the children who knew a little compared it to
> how Jesus was treated, and spoke about the naughty soldiers
> who treated Jesus badly. Mr. and Mrs Saunder' little Jesse, aged
> seven, who died on the road, said when they were stoned and
> beaten, 'They treated Jesus like this, didn't they mother?'
>
> (*Martyred Missionaries of China Inland Mission*, 21)

Another example was the martyrdom of John Philpot. In the
mid-sixteenth century, Philpot was falsely charged with heresy
and condemned to death. John Foxe described the believer's
execution on December 18, 1555:

> Coming into Smithfield he (Philpot) knelt, saying 'I will pay my
> vows in Thee, O Smithfield!' And when he reached the stake, he
> kissed it, saying 'Shall I disdain to suffer at this stake, seeing my
> Redeemer did not refuse to suffer a most vile death upon the
> cross for me?' Then he recited Psalms 106, 107, and 108, and
> prayed … They bound him to the stake, then, and the fire blazed
> up furiously; the body of John Philpot was burned to ashes.
>
> (*Foxe's Book of English Martyrs*, 275)

...strations demonstrate the fortitude and courage that ...tians can glean from the example set by Christ. Indeed, ...paved the way for us and, thus, we need not fear. As servants, we follow the Master on the beaten track.

Christians also suffer so that they would prize the cost of their salvation. When the Puritan Richard Sibbes was asked why Christians are afflicted, he said, 'I answer, we must suffer, first, that we may know what Christ suffered for us by our own experience, without which we should but lightly esteem our redemption, not knowing how to value Christ's sufferings sufficiently, which is a horrible sin, Heb. ii.3' (*Works of Richard Sibbes VI*, 162). The Apostle Paul commented, 'I count all things to be loss in view of the surpassing value of knowing Christ Jesus my Lord, for whom I have suffered ... that I may know Him, and the power of His resurrection and the fellowship of His sufferings, being conformed to His death' (Phil. 3:8, 10). If we did not suffer, in other words, we would in no way recognize or appreciate the price that Jesus paid for our redemption. (We can never completely fathom the cost of our salvation. Not only are we hindered by our sin, but we will never suffer to the degree or extent that Christ did. Our sufferings, therefore, provide us with only a hint or notion of the cost involved.)

Lastly, Christians should suffer like Jesus so that they could follow him into glory. As Calvin said, 'We share Christ's sufferings in order that as He passed from a labyrinth of all evils into heavenly glory, we may in like manner be led through various tribulations to the same glory' (*Institutes I:III:8,1*). Simply put, the cross comes before the crown (Ryle; cf. James 1:12). Paul said as much in his epistles: 'We suffer with Him in order that we may also be glorified with Him. For I consider that the sufferings of this present time are not worthy to be compared with the glory that is to be revealed to us' (Rom. 8:17-18); and, 'if we died with Him, we shall also live with Him; if we endure, we shall also reign with Him' (2 Tim. 2:11-12). Christians, then, overcome suffering and death, and they pass into the celestial city by wearing a crown of thorns and by carrying a cross of splinters. Because we bear the image of Jesus Christ we are 'more than conquerors'!

How Do We Imitate Christ When We Suffer?
The first question a Christian needs to ask when suffering is, do I in any way deserve my affliction? Have I acted in such a way that I am justly persecuted? In other words, have I been above reproach in all my actions that my trials are unjust? The Apostle Paul commented, 'By no means let any of you suffer as a murderer, or thief, or evildoer, or a troublesome meddler; but if anyone suffers as a Christian, let him not feel ashamed, but in that name let him glorify God' (1 Pet. 4:15-16).

Remember, Jesus' sufferings were undeserved. And if we are to 'share in His sufferings' we had better judge our own hearts carefully and correctly. We ought to be certain that we are not worthy of our hardships! Now and then, a Christian student complains to me of being unjustly persecuted by other students. Invariably, when I investigate further, I find that the student has often contributed in bringing persecution upon himself. That is not following the example of Christ.

If, however, we are suffering unduly in the manner of Christ, the Bible proclaims that we will be honoured. Again, note the words of Peter, 'If you are reviled for the name of Christ, you are blessed, because the Spirit of glory and God rests upon you' (1 Pet. 4:14).

In adversity, we should also strive to be like Jesus by displaying patience and longsuffering. As the Lord did not murmur or complain in His trials, His people should follow in His steps. Yet, forbearance alone is not enough. In reality, Christians are also called to glory in their sufferings. Regard the teachings of the New Testament: 'Consider it all *joy*, my brethren, when you encounter various trials' (James 1:2); and, 'to the degree that you share the sufferings of Christ keep on *rejoicing*' (1 Pet. 4:13). Christians are obligated not only to suffer patiently, but gladly too.

An attitude of joy in suffering can be a great witness to the world. For, frankly, the world does not know how to deal with suffering. It can give no reason or meaning for affliction. Why am I sick? Why did my father die? Why did I lose my job unjustly? The world can only shrug its shoulders, heave a collective sigh, and answer 'I don't know' or 'chance'. On the other hand, the beauty of the Christian message is that it gives hope and joy in the midst of great sorrow! It claims victory in the midst of death and pain! Each Christian can cheerfully proclaim with the Apostle Paul:

> Who shall separate us from the love of Christ? Shall tribulation, or distress, or persecution, or famine, or nakedness, or peril, or sword? ... But in all these things we overwhelmingly conquer through Him who loved us.
>
> (Rom. 8:35,37)

Also like Jesus, Christians suffer so that they might comfort others in distress. How true is this statement! When my father was dying of cancer, I met a Christian man in the hospital whose wife was suffering a similar death. We prayed together, and we talked about what we were both facing. What comfort, and strength we both gleaned from our time together. Observe what Paul told the Corinthian Church about his own miseries:

> Blessed be the God and Father of our Lord Jesus Christ, the father of mercies and God of all comfort; who comforts us in all our affliction so that we may be able to comfort those who are in any affliction … But if we are afflicted, it is for your comfort and salvation.
>
> (2 Cor. 1:3-4,6)

Jesus did suffer to sympathize with us, to encourage us, and to have compassion upon us (cf., Heb. 2:18; 4:15). Christians suffer also to help the brethren.

Finally, we may imitate Jesus when we suffer by realizing that our afflictions have been appointed by God. Jesus went to the cross submissively, enduring the agony, because he knew it was God's will that he suffer so. We, also, can rest assured that we have pain, misery, and grief because they have been predetermined by the eternal plan of God. We may glean great solace, perseverance, and strength that it is our heavenly Father who afflicts us. For, 'we know that God causes all things to work together for good to those who love God, to those who are called according to His purpose' (Rom. 8:28).

The Bible commands us to conform to the image of Jesus Christ (Rom. 12:2; I Peter 1:14-15). And since his principle task on earth was to suffer unto glory, we should do the same (cf., 2 Tim. 3:12). Simply put, Christians suffer so they would be like their Lord.

Dear believer, I pray that you do not lose heart in your trials and temptations. But I ask that you remember Jesus, one who suffered so dearly—indeed, never was there sorrow such as his sorrow. Yet, never was there endurance like unto his endurance. Jesus Christ conquered triumphantly by reason of his suffering! And his life was a pattern set for us to follow. May God grant you grace to persevere in your trials which leads to the gates of the heavenly city!

They whom God hath accepted in his Beloved, effectually called and sanctified by his Spirit, can neither totally nor finally fall away from the state of grace; but shall certainly persevere therein to the end, and be eternally saved.

(*Westminster Confession of Faith* Chapter XVII:1.)

There is no saint in the Bible, of whose history we have any lengthened record, who was not called to endure trouble in some form.

(J. Bowes)

6

Perseverance of the Saints

Thus far we have seen that God brings trials, tribulations, and afflictions on his people for various reasons. They may be used to prompt the believer to depend on the Lord and to turn to him in time of need. God may also refine and hone the Christian through hardships. 'Adversity is the diamond dust Heaven polishes its jewels with' (Robert Leighton). And the Christian may experience heartache and travail in order to be like Jesus, to walk his walk, and to conform to his image of righteousness. As Jonathan Edwards said,

> The way to heaven is ascending; we must be content to travel uphill, though it be hard and tiresome, and contrary to the natural bias of our flesh. We should follow Christ; the path he travelled, was the right way to heaven. We should take up our cross and follow him, in meekness and lowliness of heart, obedience and charity, diligence to do good, and patience under afflictions.
>
> (*The Christian Pilgrim*)

The Bible informs and educates Christians to the truth that they may suffer for any or all of these reasons. After all that has been covered, it is also clear that Christian suffering may take on any number of forms. It could arrive as natural disaster, or illness, or persecution, or death, or any number of different things.

One final reason for Christian affliction that we will consider is these trials may be brought upon believers in order to develop perseverance in them. Christians become stronger in their faith through adversity. How does this happen? In what manner is endurance in trials, tribulations, and adversity of benefit to the Christian?

Maturity in Faith

Patience and constancy during periods of suffering causes a believer to be a better developed Christian. Perseverance during times of trial is a means of sanctification—one becomes a healthier, holier believer. The New Testament author James put it this way: 'Consider it all joy, my brethren, when you encounter various trials, knowing that the testing of your faith produces endurance. And let endurance have its perfect result, that you may be perfect and complete, lacking nothing' (1:2-4). The Greek word the NASV translates as 'perfect', in reality, bears the meaning of 'mature.' Suffering helps to mature a believer.

The Apostle Peter concurs when he said, 'And after you have suffered for a little while, the God of all grace, who called you to his eternal glory in Christ, will himself perfect, confirm, strengthen and establish you' (1 Pet. 5:10). It is a matter of sanctification, as Paul writes to Timothy, 'And, indeed, all who desire to live godly in Christ Jesus will be persecuted' (2 Tim. 3:12). Trials, afflictions, and testings are the lot of the

Christian. The one who endures them with patience will be a more godly, holy person.

Proof of Faith

Firmness and tenacity during times of trial are confirmation of one's faith in Christ. Peter declared, 'In this you greatly rejoice, even though now for a little while, if necessary, you have been distressed by various trials, that the proof of your faith, being more precious than gold which is perishable, even though tested by fire, may be found to result in praise and glory and honor at the revelation of Jesus Christ' (1 Pet. 1:6-7). Endurance is an indication of one being a good soldier of Christ. Paul told Timothy, 'Suffer hardship with me, as a good soldier of Christ Jesus' (2 Tim. 2:3). It is clear evidence that one is indeed in God's service: as the Apostle wrote to the Corinthian church, 'giving no cause for offense in anything, in order that the ministry be not discredited, but in everything commending ourselves as servants of God, in much endurance, in afflictions, in hardships, in distresses, in beatings, in imprisonments, in tumults, in labors, in sleeplessness, in hunger' (2 Cor. 6:3-5).

Suffering can be for the testing of Christians (1 Pet. 4:12-13). And when believers persevere in it, it is a sure indication of their worthiness for the kingdom of God. Paul explained in regard to the tenacious character of the suffering Thessalonian church: 'We speak proudly of you among the churches of God for your perseverance and faith in the midst of all your persecutions and afflictions which you endure. This is a plain indication of God's righteous judgment so that you may be considered worthy of the kingdom of God, for which indeed you are suffering' (2 Thess. 1:4-5). It is proof that one loves Christ, that one belongs to him, and that he is strengthening one to be patient and long-suffering in the midst of trial.

A Witness of Faith

When a Christian endures pain and suffering, it may aid other believers who are in affliction. One realizes that one is not travelling alone through the slough of despond or the valley of the shadow of death. Paul wrote to the Corinthian church, 'But if we are afflicted, it is for your comfort and salvation; or if we are comforted, it is for your comfort, which is effective in the patient enduring of the same sufferings which we also suffer; and our hope for you is firmly grounded, knowing that as you are sharers of our sufferings, so also you are sharers of our comfort' (2 Cor. 1:6-7).

Thus, we need to understand that patient suffering is a good witness to others in the church, and that we do not suffer alone. 'But resist him [*the devil*], firm in your faith, knowing that the same experiences of suffering are being accomplished by your brethren who are in the world' (1 Pet. 5:9).

Perplexity of the World

A Christian's patience in trial also sends a message to the unbelieving world. It can send adversaries into confusion who are amazed and wonder when they see the courage and comfort of the saints during times of trial. For example, 'Luctantius boasts of the braveness of the martyrs of his time: "Our children and women, not to speak of men, do in silence overcome their tormentors, and the fire cannot so much as fetch a sigh from them"' (Brooks, *Complete Works*, vol. 2, 357). Endurance in trial can, in the final analysis, defeat God's enemies. Thomas Brooks tells the story of Vincentius:

> Vincentius, who by his patience and constancy madded his tormentors; wherefore they stripped him stark naked, whipped his body all over to a gore blood, sprinkled salt and vinegar over all his wounds, set his feet on burning coals, then cast

him naked into a loathsome dungeon, the pavement whereof was sharp shells, and his bed to lie on a bundle of thorns. All which this blessed martyr received, without so much as a groan, breathing out his spirit in these words, 'Vincentius is my name, and by the grace of God I will still be Vincentius, in spite of all your torments.' Persecution brings death in one hand and life in the other; for while it kills the body it crowns the soul.

(Complete Works, vol. 2, 356)

Fortitude in trial, even unto death, can also be an evangelistic witness to a dying world. One example comes from the time of the Boxer Rebellion in China at the opening turn of the twentieth century. Christian missionaries and natives were undergoing severe persecution and much martyrdom at this time. Mrs. Bryson tells the story of a young Chinese man that she had just recently baptized. His older brother had been killed and mutilated by the Boxers. She comments,

It was when he found such calm trust in Christ, and deter-mination to cling to Him even at the cost of his life, on the part of his brother, that he decided there must be something in the religion of Jesus which he had never known before. So he came to Christ.

(Cross and Crown, 158)

Improvement in One's Work for Christ
William Carey, the well-known missionary to India, spent much of his time translating, publishing, and distributing biblical literature throughout the various provinces of that land. Due to his supporters in England, he was able to procure a building to hold printing presses and the grammars and dictionaries that he had written himself of the native language. It was a wonderful, faithful, and time-consuming part of Carey's missionary work. One day while he was away,

a fire broke out and destroyed the building and all its contents. Everything was gone: the presses, the building, the Bibles, and all Carey's manuscripts upon which he had laboured for years.

When Carey returned to the mission station, he was told about the loss. 'Without a word of despair or anger he knelt down and thanked God that he had the strength to do the work all over again. He started immediately, not wasting a moment in idle despair and before his death he duplicated his first achievements and produced far better work than he had done formerly' (*Christian Victory*).

Suffering can make our work and ministry for Christ better. It can refine our work and polish it. It can cause us to produce better fruit when we endure our loss or affliction. The pruning of trees may be a fit analogy. Each year the gardener takes a knife to the trees, cutting and lopping off branches. The trees endure, and do not cry out! And through that process the trees produce better fruit. May we see that our suffering as believers can have the same result, and may we pray that God would use our suffering to produce better fruit in us and from us.

Training for Glory

Endurance in suffering prepares us for heaven. It demonstrates that this world, with its ways and pleasures, is quickly gone. It tears us from the world and places our eyes on glory. It clears up the mists of this world that we may see the true heavenly city. James declared, 'Blessed is a man who perseveres under trial; for once he has been approved, he will receive the crown of life, which the Lord has promised to those who love him' (James 1:12). The cross comes before the crown! And 'by your endurance you will gain your souls' (Luke 21:19).

John Flavel encourages us in this matter: 'Good souls, hold fast, if ever you hope to possess the glory that is here, hold fast, Gal. vi 9. Mat. x 22. Rev. iii 12, 21. Rev. xxi 7' (*The Works of John Flavel*, vol. IV, 519). The Christian's true reward and inheritance is yet to come, and suffering may help us to see the heavenly prize with crystal clear eyes. Peter told the suffering church of his day, 'Beloved, do not be surprised at the fiery ordeal among you, which comes upon you for your testing, as though some strange thing were happening to you; but to the degree that you share the sufferings of Christ, keep on rejoicing; so that also at the revelation of his glory, you may rejoice with exultation' (1 Pet. 4:12-13).

Thus, when the believer endures his suffering it is partly because of hope in what God has done and the eternal rest that has been secured for him. Paul said, 'And not only this, but we also exult in our tribulations, knowing that tribulation brings about perseverance; and perseverance, proven character; and proven character, hope; and hope does not disappoint, because the love of God has been poured out within our hearts through the Holy Spirit who was given to us' (Rom. 5:3-5). Hope in the New Testament is not wishful thinking, but it is assurance. And hope 'does not disappoint,' but it brings about what is the right and true result.

Keeping the Promise
Persistence in trial and affliction is one of the means by which God has ordained that his people would receive what he has promised to them. The author to the Hebrews explained to the suffering church of his day why they have undergone such 'conflicts of suffering': it is because it has a 'great reward' (10:35). He continued, 'For you have need of endurance, so that when you have done the will of God, you may receive what was promised' (10:36). Abraham, for example, endured much in his life 'living as an alien in the land of promise, as

in a foreign land, dwelling in tents' (11:9). He did, however, have the promise of God that he would be blessed, have many descendants, and the land would belong to him and his seed. 'And thus, having patiently waited, he obtained the promise' (6:15). And what he gained was an eternal, imperishable land that will never fade away, a heavenly inheritance and reward that is never-ending, and a seed that will live there forever.

Endurance through suffering to the end reaps the greatest rewards. Jesus said, 'And you will be hated by all on account of my name, but it is the one who has endured to the end who will be saved' (Matt. 10:22; Mark 13:13).

God's Glory

The opening question of the Shorter Catechism is, what is the chief end of man? The answer is, man's chief end is to glorify God, and to enjoy him forever. There are no qualifications to that answer. It does not matter what one's race is, or gender, or socioeconomic status, or age, or whatever; one is to have as one's purpose in life to glorify the Heavenly Father. The Scriptures tell us that when a believer endures hardship it is a graphic means of glorifying God. Peter told the church, 'If you are reviled for the name of Christ, you are blessed, because the Spirit of glory and of God rests upon you … if anyone suffers as a Christian, let him not feel ashamed, but in that name let him glorify God' (1 Pet. 4:14, 16).

The glory of God is the ultimate purpose of a believer's suffering and perseverance. In John 9:1-3, we read the following account:

> And as he passed by, he saw a man blind from birth. And his disciples asked him, 'Rabbi, who sinned, this man or his parents, that he should be born blind?' Jesus answered, 'It was neither that this man sinned, nor his parents; but it was in order that the works of God might be displayed in him.'

No matter what the source, however, most Christians react to suffering in more or less the same way: either bitter resentment or lugubrious silence. Moreover, some Christians seem to take morbid pleasure from their having to 'bear a cross,' as they put it. They are at great pains to point out how noble they are to bear so patiently with such misfortune.

(F. Steele, *The Privilege of Suffering*)

In contrast, it is surprising how so many of the passages we have considered in this chapter rather speak of joy and exultation that should accompany Christian suffering. And, thus, not only is the Christian to endure hardship, but he is to do it with a joyful heart! Paul proclaimed, 'Let us also exult in our tribulations ...' (Rom. 5:3); and James said, 'And we should consider it all joy, my brethren, when you encounter various trials ...' (James 1:2); and Peter said, 'In this you greatly rejoice ...' (1 Pet. 1:6) and 'keep on rejoicing' (1 Pet. 4:13) in the midst of persecution and pain. But how can this be? How can I be joyful in times of hardship? How can I endure and be joyful at the same time?

The first thing that we need to understand is that endurance and joy during times of suffering are not something that we can call up from our inner selves. It is not picking ourselves up by our boot-strings and having a stiff upper lip. These are not feelings or senses that are natural to fallen humanity. Despair and hopelessness are the natural responses of the world to suffering. So where do endurance and joy come from? They are fruit of the Spirit: 'But the fruit of the Spirit is love, joy, peace, patience, kindness, goodness, faithfulness, gentleness, self-control; against such things there is no law' (Gal. 5:22-3; cf. Col. 1:11). The reality is that 'only he can give me joy ...' (K. Olsen, *Notes on Sorrow and Joy*), and only he can give me a long-suffering, steadfast heart in the midst of trial. As David said, it is Yahweh who 'hast turned for me my mourning into dancing' and 'hast loosed my sackcloth and girded me with gladness' (Ps. 30:11).

David, in the midst of great trials, prayed to God that he would be joyful even in the midst of pain and anguish. In regard to the trying circumstances surrounding the sin with Bathsheba and David's penitence, he said, 'Make me to hear joy and gladness, let the bones which thou hast broken rejoice' (Ps. 51:8). And later in the same psalm, David petitions God with 'Restore to me the joy of thy salvation' (v. 12).

Christ himself set a wonderful example of being perseverant and joyful when undergoing trying times. The author to the Hebrews said that Christians ought to fix 'our eyes on Jesus, the author and perfecter of faith, who for the joy set before him endured the cross, despising the shame, and has sat down at the right hand of the throne of God. For consider him who has endured such hostility by sinners against himself, so that you may not grow weary and lose heart' (12:2-3). And we ought to imitate Paul, in the same way that Timothy was commended for following him: 'But you followed my teaching, conduct, purpose, faith, patience, love, perseverance, persecutions, and sufferings, such as happened to me at Antioch, at Iconium and at Lystra; what persecutions I endured, and out of them all the Lord delivered me!' (2 Tim. 3:10-11). And, indeed, in the final analysis, the Christian endures suffering because it always ends in the Lord's mercy and compassion. 'Behold, we count those blessed who endured. You have heard of the endurance of Job and have seen the outcome of the Lord's dealings, that the Lord is full of compassion and is merciful' (James 5:11).

The Christian is called to run the race of life with endurance and fortitude. We are not to lose heart or shrink from our task. Flavel said, 'The upright soul abhors to flinch from his duty, let come on him what will' (*The Works of John Flavel*, vol. iv, 519). Scripture encourages us to 'run with endurance the race that is set before us' (Heb. 12:1). The course may be long, treacherous, and uphill, but that does not matter. For we do not run the race in our own power, but 'I can do all things through him who strengthens me' (Phil. 4:13).

Part III:

Why Do Unbelievers Suffer?

So I have known some persons reclaimed from the unfruitful works of darkness, by violent and severe means. The Almighty addressed their stubborn hearts as he addressed the Israelites at Sinai, with lightning in his eyes, and thunder in his voice. The conscience, smitten with a sense of guilt and apprehension of eternal vengeance, trembled through all her powers; just as that strong mountain tottered to its center, pangs of remorse and agonies of fear preceded their new birth. They were reduced to their last extremities, almost overwhelmed with despair, before they found rest in Jesus Christ.

(R. Salter)

All those whom God hath predestinated unto life, and those only, he is pleased, in his appointed and accepted time, effectually to call, by his Word and Spirit, out of that state of sin and death, in which they are by nature, to grace and salvation by Jesus Christ; enlightening their minds spiritually and savingly, to understand the things of God … effectually drawing them to Jesus Christ, yet so as they come most freely, being made willing by his grace.

(*Westminster Confession of Faith*, Chapter X:1.)

7

SUFFERING AS FOREWARNING

God brings unbelievers out of a state of death and darkness into the marvellous light of the knowledge of Jesus Christ through various means. Sometimes his call and work are mild, and he applies the truth to their hearts by a still small voice. As R. Salter comments, 'The kingdom of God took place in their souls, without noise or observation. They passed from death unto life, from a carnal to a regenerate state, by almost imperceptible advances. The transition resembled the growth of corn: was very visible when effected, though scarcely sensible while accomplishing.' How many we know in Protestantism who hold zealously to the doctrines of grace and are regenerated, yet they are unable to detail the time or event of conversion! There is no doubt of conversion in these cases, but God walked softly with them and quietly brought them into the kingdom.

In others, God speaks primarily to the intellect. The Christian author C. S. Lewis tells of his own conversion that he had been changed from atheism to Christianity by an intellectual process. Lewis remarks, 'In the Trinity term of 1929 I gave in, and admitted that God is God, and knelt and prayed: perhaps, that night, the most dejected and reluctant convert in all England. I did not then see what is now the most shining and obvious thing; the Divine humility which will accept a convert even on such terms … The hardness of God is kinder than the softness of men, and His compulsion is our liberation' (*Surprised by Joy*, 215).

To some, the impulses of grace appear suddenly, like a flash of lightning, with no thought having been given to it. A person may be engaged in another duty altogether, but God unexpectedly opens his heart to the truths of the gospel. Such was the case with the sons of Zebedee who were mending their nets (Mark 1:19-20), and with Matthew who was busy at his work of the tax house (Mark 2:14). Jesus simply said to them, 'Follow me,' and they immediately obeyed as their hearts were changed.

God may use suffering as a means to warn the unbeliever and to bring him to repentance. In other words, God's judgements, which can be displayed by affliction, can serve as a sign to unbelievers and induce them to faith. There are many examples of this means of conversion, but we will consider only a few at this time.

John Newton (1725–1807)

Until March 10, 1748, John Newton was a seaman, and a proud, violent blasphemer. He was a rebel and an atheist. His tongue was so full of poison and vile cursing that even tough, hard-bitten sailors were shocked by his rantings. But on the evening before that fateful day, the ship on which Newton was serving, the *Greyhound*, was struck by a violent sea and it began to sink. It was so bad that one of the sailors fell overboard to his death. Thus, the violent man was struck by a violent storm.

Newton first responded by trying to be courageous as he and others worked the pumps. He even cavalierly shouted, 'In a few days this disaster will serve us to talk of, over a glass of wine!' His companions were not so sure, and some of them prepared themselves for death. After four hours at the pumps, Newton was exhausted and was losing heart. Out of the depths of his soul Newton uttered the words, 'If this will not do, the Lord have mercy on us!' Instantly, Newton was struck by the force of his own words. Unpremeditated, this was the first desire for mercy that he had breathed 'for the space of many years'. At once it occurred to him: 'What mercy can there be for me?—the ship's chief blasphemer, the loudest swearer, the man who mocked the Lord's existence—*What mercy can there be for me?*' (Pollock, *Amazing Grace*, 74).

On the next day, the sea grew more violent and Newton feared for his life. He thought 'if the Christian religion was true I could not be forgiven.' After hour upon hour of storm, the ship was finally clear and free of water. Newton believed that they had been saved by the hand of God, and perhaps he could find the way to forgiveness. He began praying and reading the New Testament, and he concluded:

> The more I looked at what Jesus had done on the cross, the more He met my case exactly. I needed someone or something to stand between a righteous God and my sinful self: a God who must punish sins and blasphemies, and myself, who had wallowed in both to the neck. I needed an Almighty Saviour who should step in and take my sins away, and I found such a one in the New Testament.

Once Newton understood this, he repented and believed on the Lord Jesus Christ. Thus, was Newton's conversion.

Newton was vividly aware that God used affliction as a means of his salvation. He once commented, 'Afflictive dispensations are likewise of his sending. And the consideration of his hand in them, the good he designs us by them, the assurance we have of being supported under them, and brought through them …' (*Works*, vol. 2, 432). Newton once wrote the following to a parishioner who had two very sick children:

> Upon the same grounds, if either of your children should be removed, I shall not so directly ascribe it to the illness, as to the will of God; for, if, upon the whole, it be the most for his glory, and best for you, they likewise shall recover. Should he appoint otherwise, it must be best, because he does it … Farther, the Lord is not only sovereign, but infinitely wise and good; and therefore it is our interest, as well as our duty, to acquiesce in his appointments.
>
> (*Works*, vol. 6, 192–3.)

Newton knew that he was 'a brand plucked from the burning' and that God had placed him in the furnace to become one of his own.

Robert Murray McCheyne

Rev. Robert Murray McCheyne died at the young age of twenty-nine years, but certainly not without hope. On his death bed McCheyne gave thanks to God 'for strength in the time of weakness—for light in the time of darkness—for you in the time of sorrow—for comforting us in all our tribulations, that we may be able to comfort those that are in any trouble, by the comfort wherewith we ourselves are comforted by God.' Despite his few years, McCheyne's impact on the church in Scotland in his day was tremendous. And his influence on the church universal has been staggering, especially as his life was portrayed in Andrew Bonar's *Memoir and Remains of the Rev. Robert Murray McCheyne* (1844).

McCheyne's call to repentance and the changing of his heart began with trial. When he was eighteen years old, his brother David 'fell asleep in Jesus.' And the 'death of this brother, with all its circumstances, was used by the Holy Spirit to produce a deep impression on Robert's mind' (Bonar, 23). And, as Bonar concludes, 'There can be no doubt that the death of his eldest brother, David, was the event which awoke him from the sleep of nature, and brought in the first beam of divine light into his soul. By that providence the Lord was calling one soul to enjoy the treasures of grace, while he took the other into the possession of glory' (pp. 22–3).

McCheyne's diary has numerous allusions to the death of his brother and its impact on the young McCheyne. On the one year anniversary of his brother's death, he wrote, 'On this morning last year came the first overwhelming blow to my worldliness; how blessed to me, Thou, O God, only knowest, who hast made it so.' Years later, McCheyne wrote to a friend, 'Pray for me, that I may be made holier and wiser—less like myself, and more like my heavenly Master; that I may not regard my life, if so be I may finish my course with joy. This day eleven years ago, I lost my loved and loving brother, and began to seek a Brother who cannot die.' David McCheyne had died on July 8, 1831; Robert would be dead in less than a year after he made this last entry into his diary (March 21, 1843).

The Plague of 1665

Thomas Vincent (1634–78) provides an account of a virulent and deadly plague that engulfed the city of London in 1665. His book is entitled *God's Terrible Voice in the City*. He describes in graphic detail how thousands of Londoners died that year from the sickness. For example, during a particularly heavy month of death, he says:

Now the cloud is very black, and the storm comes down upon us very sharp. Now Death rides triumphantly on his pale horse through our streets; and breaks into every house almost, where any inhabitants are found. Now people fall as thick as leaves from the trees in autumn, when they are shaken by a mighty wind ... Now in some places where the people did generally stay, not one house in a hundred but is infected; and in many houses half the family is swept away; in some the whole, from the eldest to the youngest; few escape with the death of but one or two; never did so many husbands and wives die together; never did so many parents carry their children with them to the grave ...

It is heart-wrenching to read Vincent's account of thousands perishing. It was a dark and terrible time for residents of London.

Yet, much as in the day of Joel (the locust plague in chapter 1), God used the plague in London to warn people of impending doom, and to bring some of them to saving grace in Jesus Christ. It was not all bleak. Vincent tells of faithful gospel-preaching ministers who stayed or came to London to serve the people. 'Now they are preaching,' Vincent remarks, 'and every sermon was unto them, as if they were preaching their last.' The response was electrifying. Vincent comments on the people's response:

If you ever saw a drowning man catch at a rope, you may guess how eagerly many people did catch at the Word, when they were ready to be overwhelmed by this overflowing scourge, which was passing through the city; when death was knocking at so many doors; and God was crying aloud by his judgments; and ministers were now sent to knock, cry aloud, and lift up their voice like a trumpet: then the people began to open the ear and the heart, which were fast shut and barred before ... Great were the impressions which the Word made upon many hearts ... Now the net is cast, and many fishes are taken, the pool is moved by the angel, and many leprous spirits, and sin-sick souls, are cured: many were brought to the birth, and I hope not a few were born again ...

Yes, God used this severe trial of an on-going plague to bring many people to a saving knowledge through his grace. Grace in the midst of judgement! Indeed, the Lord employs many different circumstances to prompt people to faith (and they hear the preached word), and one of these is suffering.

Thief on the Cross

Although it appears to be a less common divine intervention than what we have seen above, God uses suffering to graciously call some at the hour of death. The thief on the cross (Luke 23:39-43) is a good example of this 'rare miracle of mercy' (William Guthrie, *The Christian's Saving Interest*, 46). This criminal's conversion is confirmed by the remarkable circumstances of his conversation with the other thief and with Jesus. First, the man recognizes and confesses his own sin, guilt, and worthiness of condemnation (v. 41). He then seeks and asks for the Saviour's intervention (v. 42). In his request, he acknowledges the kingship of Jesus. And, finally, he receives the promise of the Saviour that after death he will live in Paradise with Jesus (v. 43).

Luke purposefully sets a contrast between the two thieves. The second criminal is unrepentant, and he blasphemes Jesus as were many standing near to the cross of Christ (vv. 35, 39). The point of the contrast is poignantly summarized by J. C. Ryle: 'There was only one dying thief saved, that none may despair and that none may presume.'

Earl Fitzhardinge (d. 1857), the lord of Berkeley, became a Christian on his deathbed. At a particular business meeting that he was attending, the Earl was spoken to by Rev. Morton Brown. The minister confronted him by saying, 'I hope, my lord, you will forgive me, but I feel constrained, as a Christian minister, to observe that you yourself have a soul to be saved or lost.' The Earl never forgot that remark, and when he became deathly ill he sent for the minister—the only man who ever spoke to him about the state of his soul. He was converted, and he died in Christian triumph. On his deathbed he proclaimed, 'All is peace! All is right! I had always thought religion was a melancholy thing, but I now find it is the only thing worth living for. Here am I, a poor penitent sinner, clinging to the cross of Christ.'

According to reports, Steve McQueen, the Hollywood actor, called on Billy Graham not long before he died of cancer in Bakersfield, California. He said, 'Billy, I'm dying and I don't have eternal life. How can I be sure that I have eternal life?' The evangelist shared the words of Jesus with him, 'My sheep hear my voice, and I know them, and they follow me; and I give eternal life to them, and they shall never perish; and no one shall snatch them our of my hand' (John 10:27-28). McQueen died on November 7, 1980 at the age of fifty. An open Bible lay across his chest and Steve McQueen lay in death with a smile on his face.

As stated above, deathbed conversions are uncommon provisions of grace from above. In his comments on Proverbs 1:24-26, William Guthrie says, 'This Scripture, although it does not shut mercy's door upon any one who at the hour of death do sincerely judge themselves and flee to Christ, as this penitent thief did; yet it certainly implieth that very few, who reject the offer until then, are honoured with repentance as he was. Their cry, as not being sincere, and of the right stamp, shall not be heard' (*The Christian's Saving Interest*, 46). One should not wait, having in mind that I will wait until that day when I am on my deathbed and it is needed. One should turn now to Christ in repentance and belief.

Ultimately, of course, it is the work of the Holy Spirit in one's heart that brings a person to saving faith and belief in Jesus Christ. As Peter Toon remarks, 'However we may define the new birth, it clearly occurs in the human soul through the action of the Spirit of the living God ... The Spirit who regenerates the individual and who creates the new people of God is the same Spirit who came upon (and remains upon) Jesus the Messiah' (*Born Again: A Biblical and Theological Study of Regeneration*, 16). That is a true statement; yet, we need to recognize that the circumstances that the Holy Spirit uses in conversion varies greatly. At times, it may be more gradual and serene, but at other times, it may be more violent and due to hardship and suffering. Some are pricked in the heart (Acts 2:37), and some tremble (Acts 16:29). The Philippian jailer had great anguish and was one who 'trembled with fear'; he was at the end of his rope and, thus, asked Paul, 'What must I do to be saved?' (Acts 16:30).

Christians need to be aware and alert to the sufferings of unbelievers. These times can be particularly advantageous and fruitful for evangelism. Suffering tends to focus one's mind and heart on one's own constitution, condition, and nature. When Paul reflects on the conversion of many in the Corinthian church, he says, 'I now rejoice, not that you were made sorrowful, but that you were made sorrowful to the point of repentance; for you were made sorrowful according to the will of God, in order that you might not suffer loss in anything through us. For the sorrow that is according to the will of God produces a repentance without regret, leading to salvation; but the sorrow of the world produces death' (2 Cor. 7:9-10). May God continue to use suffering in the lives of unbelievers to bring them to a sense of sin and need of repentance before the holy God.

Will God let man get by with such disobedience and defection? Certainly not, for the wrath of God is revealed from heaven, both against our inborn sinfulness and our actual sins, and he will punish them according to his righteous judgment in time and in eternity, as he declared: 'Cursed be everyone who does not abide by all things written in the book of the Law, and do them.'

(*Heidelberg Catechism*, Question 10.)

There are the black clouds of God's wrath now hanging directly over your heads, full of the dreadful storm, and big with thunder; and were it not for the restraining hand of God, it would immediately burst forth upon you. The sovereign pleasure of God, for the present, stays his rough wind; otherwise it would come like a whirl-wind, and you would be like chaff of the summer threshing floor.

(Jonathan Edwards, *Sinners in the Hands of an Angry God.*)

8

Suffering as Condemnation

Because of sin, all men deserve God's condemnation. We have all earned death (Rom. 6:23) and we are deserving of God's wrath coming upon us. God is a just judge and, therefore, he requires that his justice be satisfied. Mankind must pay the price for rebellion against God. People must be punished for their sins.

Yet, it is a right thing to say that God loves all people. That is a strong statement that is in need of qualification. He does love everyone in a general way. Macleod puts it this way: 'God's general love for the human race confers upon mankind a vast array of precious blessings: the sun shines, the rain falls and we enjoy all the benefits of art, science and technology, of affluence, of global fecundity, of human friendship and love and all the preciousness of human relationships' (A Faith to Live By, 45). Such is the love that God has for all men. However, there is a love on God's part that goes way beyond those mere temporal benefits: it is a salvific love that only belongs to God's elect, to those whom he specially set apart for his redeeming love. It is a deep, particular, and personal love that God has for his people.

Thus, there are two types of people on the earth: the elect, the ones upon whom God lavishes his redeeming love (Eph. 1:3-4), and the non-elect, those upon whom God bestows his general love but not his salvific love. The manner in which God bountifully gives his redeeming love to the elect is through the work of his son Jesus Christ (John 3:16; 1 Pet. 1:18-19). Christ died for the elect of God. And a primary purpose of his death was to be a substitution for the elect and thereby take upon himself the condemnation and curse that belonged to the elect of God. As the Apostle Paul remarks, 'Christ redeemed us from the curse of the law, having become a curse for us' (Gal. 3:13). Thus, because of the work of Christ, believers are freed from the condemnation of God that is so rightly deserved. This is truly amazing grace! One major consequence of this gospel message is the fact that when a Christian suffers or is afflicted it is never for the purpose of condemnation or destruction. Such things are always for the good and benefit of the Christian; they are for restoration. 'And we know that God causes all things to work together for good to those who love God, to those who are called according to his purpose' (Rom. 8:28).

The same can not be said of unbelievers. For the non-elect, there is no reprieve from the condemnation of God. Unbelievers are deserving of the wrath of God (Col. 3:5-6). There is no repentance on their part, but they are hardened in their sin. They do evil wilfully and maliciously. And they have no mediator, and no one to stand between them and God, and no one to take on their deserved condemnation.

One consequence of this reality is that temporal suffering is condemnatory and preparatory. It is not for restoration but for punishment.

Temporal Suffering
The non-elect are 'vessels of wrath prepared for destruction' (Rom. 9:22). The 'wrath of God abides' on them (John 3:36). Jonathan Edwards defined their position on earth in the sermon title 'Sinners in the Hands of an Angry God.' They are 'by nature children of wrath' (Eph. 2:3). God's wrath may come on unbelievers here on earth in the form of suffering, calamity, and affliction. These earthly troubles thus may serve as signs of judgement on non-Christians. The author of Proverbs says about the wicked:

> A worthless person, a wicked man,
>   Is the one who walks with a false mouth,
>   Who winks with his eyes,
>   Who signals with his feet,
>   Who points with his fingers;
>   Who with perversity in his heart
>   devises evil continually,
>   Who spreads strife.
>   Therefore his calamity will come suddenly;
>   Instantly he will be broken,
>   and there will be no healing.
>
> (6:12-15)

Indeed, the promised wrath of God may come on the unbeliever here on earth as judgement. This much is clear. Paul says that 'the wrath of God is revealed from heaven against all ungodliness and unrighteousness of men…' (Rom. 1:18).

Biblical examples of God's wrath on unrepentant sinners in this world are many. Thus, for example, the flood of Noah's day came on mankind because 'the LORD saw that the wickedness of man was great on the earth, and that every intent of the thoughts of his heart was only evil continually' (Gen. 6:5). Affliction, in this instance, in the form of death and destruction, happened on the earth because of mankind's earned and deserved condemnation. When the Ashdodites house the captured ark of God in the temple of Dagon, God brings great suffering on them for their wickedness. The text reads, 'Now the hand of the LORD was heavy on the Ashdodites, and he ravaged them and smote them with tumors, both Ashdod and its territories' (1 Sam. 5:6). In Egypt, God brought great calamities on the Egyptians because they wickedly oppressed the people of Israel (Ps. 78:43-51). Pharaoh was a particular target of God's wrath and indignation because of his refusal to let the children of Israel leave Egypt (Exod. 4:23; 10:3).

Often God's temporal judgement of an unbeliever takes the form of ironic justice, that is, the very form of an unbeliever's earthly judgement is based on his own heinous activity. In Psalm 9:15-16, David lays down the fundamental principle of ironic justice. He says:

> The nations have sunk down in the pit
>   which they have made;
> In the net which they hid,
>   their own foot has been caught.
> The LORD has made himself known;
>   He has executed judgement.
> In the work of his own hands
>   the wicked is snared.

Ironic justice is a form of dramatic irony in which the force of a person's actions or words result in an outcome opposite of what was intended. In 2 Chronicles 26, Uzziah is pictured as profaning and desecrating the temple. As a result of his activity, Uzziah, in an ironic fashion, is struck with leprosy. The text says, 'The LORD had smitten him' (v. 20). By God's actions, Uzziah himself becomes profane and desecrated. In the Book of Esther, the evil Haman is ironically hung on the very gallows that he had built to hang Mordechai (7:10).

Even the event of the crucifixion bears a sense of ironic justice. There Satan and his minions crucify the son of God; yet it is that very event that causes and signals their defeat. Through his death and resurrection, Christ soundly conquers the evil one and his followers.

God's wrath on the unregenerate here on earth can be fierce. In regard to the Egyptians during the exodus period, the psalmist says,

> He sent upon them his burning anger,
>   Fury, and indignation, and trouble,
>   A band of destroying angels.
>
> (Ps. 78:49).

Because the Amalekites had set themselves against the Hebrews during the wilderness wanderings, God later commanded Saul to 'go and strike Amalek and utterly destroy all that he has, and do not spare him' (1 Sam. 15:2-3). This destruction is called 'his [i.e., the Lord's] fierce wrath' (1 Sam. 28:18).

The reality is, however, that the punishment that the unregenerate experience here on earth is a mere foretaste of what is to come. In other words, suffering, affliction, disease, and death are mere sips of the full drink of eternal death for the non-Christian. They are merely preparatory for what may be expected for eternity. This is a hard thing, yet Scripture makes it clear that it is a true thing.

Eternal Suffering

Paul describes the future of the unbeliever in this way: 'But because of your stubbornness and unrepentant heart you are storing up wrath for yourself in the day of wrath and revelation of the righteous judgement of God, who will render to every man according to his deeds' (Rom. 2:5-6). This eternal punishment and suffering that comes from God's wrath is *certain*. Paul explains: 'Let no one deceive you with empty words, for because of these things [i.e., sin] the wrath of God comes upon the sons of disobedience' (Eph. 5:6). And he says in Colossians, 'Therefore consider the members of your earthly body as dead to immorality, impurity, passion, evil desire, and greed, which amounts to idolatry. For it is on account of these things that the wrath of God will come' (3:5-6). For the non-elect, there is no holding it back; it is a torrent that will come. The unbeliever will one day suffer the infinite weight and power of God's fury.

It is an *eternal*, everlasting suffering. This truth is interpreted by Jonathan Edwards in his most famous sermon:

> It would be dreadful to suffer this fierceness and wrath of Almighty God one moment; but you must suffer it to all eternity. There will be no end to this exquisite horrible misery. When you look forward, you shall see a long for ever, a boundless duration before you, which will swallow up your thoughts, and amaze your soul; and you will absolutely despair of ever having any deliverance, any end, any mitigation, any rest at all. You will know certainly that you must wear out long ages, millions of millions of ages, in wrestling and conflicting with this almighty merciless vengeance; and then when you have done so, when so many ages have actually been spent by you in this manner, you will know that all is but a point to what remains. So that your punishment will indeed be infinite.
>
> (*Sinners in the Hands of an Angry God*)

The Westminster Confession of Faith says that 'the wicked, who know not God, and obey not the gospel of Jesus Christ, shall be cast into eternal torments, and be punished with everlasting destruction from the presence of the Lord, and from the glory of his power' (XXXIII:2). In regard to the final judgement, Jesus teaches 'And these will go away into eternal punishment, but the righteous into eternal life' (Matt. 25:46).

Like temporal suffering, eternal suffering is the result of the *fierce* wrath of God. Yet, the former pales in comparison to the latter. *The Scots Confession* puts it this way: 'the reprobate and unfaithful departed have anguish, torment, and pain which cannot be expressed' (XVII). John calls this judgement on the wicked 'the wine press of the fierce wrath of God' (Rev. 19:15). Regarding this verse, Edwards deserves to be quoted again:

> The words are exceeding terrible. If it had only been said, 'the wrath of God,' the words would have implied that which is infinitely dreadful: but it is 'the fierceness and wrath of God.' The fury of God! The fierceness of Jehovah! Oh, how dreadful must that be! Who can utter or conceive what such expressions carry in them!
>
> (*Sinners in the Hands of an Angry God*)

Finally, we need to recognize that the eternal suffering of the non-elect is the result of the judgement of God. It is a consequence of the wrath of the infinite God. This is a fearsome and terrible thing. And it ought to invoke awe in humanity. Jesus taught that when he said, 'And I say to you, my friends, do not be afraid of those who kill the body, and after that have no more that they can do. But I will warn you whom to fear: fear the One who after he has killed has authority to cast into hell; yes, I tell you, fear him!' (Luke 12:4-5).

The wrath of God coming on an unbeliever in the form of eternal punishment is a difficult matter. But we must understand that it is a *deserved* end. The Westminster Confession of Faith states that 'Every sin, both original and actual, being a transgression of the righteous law of God, and contrary thereunto, doth, in its own nature, bring guilt upon the sinner, whereby he is bound over to the wrath of God, and curse of the law, and so made subject to death, with all miseries spiritual, temporal, and eternal' (VI:6). Sin simply leads to death, in all its forms. Without a mediator or deliverer the end result is a foregone conclusion with no reprieve.

The Only Answer
The elect are saved by works. However, it is not by their own works or merit that they are delivered from condemnation and eternal suffering. For mankind is enslaved to sin. And this state of sin extends to all areas of mankind's being and life: it is the all-pervasiveness of sin. Therefore, Paul concludes that all people in their natural state are 'dead in their (lit. 'your') trespasses and sins' (Eph. 2:1). Indeed, 'the wages of sin is death' (Rom. 6:23). And as dead men they are in a helpless condition. They are unable to save themselves from the wrath to come. They are unable to choose God and his ways. They are only able to act as dead people. To the point, the Scriptures teach that people are dead in their sins, totally depraved, and they have no ability or inclination to save themselves even if it was offered to them.

Clearly then, humans can not be saved by their own good works or merit. If a person is ever to be delivered from just condemnation, it must be the work of God. Through God's efforts people can be born again and raised from the dead. And since it is God's initiative and God's work, then it must be his choice regarding who are to be rescued from judgement. Paul summarizes this thought in his epistle to the Romans:

> What shall we say then? There is no injustice with God, is there? May it never be! For he says to Moses, 'I will have mercy on whom I have mercy, and I will have compassion on whom I have compassion.' So then it does not depend on the man who wills or the man who runs, but on God who has mercy. For the Scripture says to Pharaoh, 'For this very purpose I raised you up, to demonstrate my power in you, and that my name might be proclaimed throughout the whole earth.' So then he has mercy on whom he desires, and he hardens whom he desires.
>
> (9:14-18)

The context of Paul's statement is his definition of who is and how one becomes a believer, one who has been justified by the work of God (Rom. 1:16-17).

The means by which God delivers the elect is by the sacrifice of Jesus Christ on the cross (John 1:29; Heb. 10:14). In that death, the sinless redeemer took on the sins and curses due his people. Although he deserved none of it, he took the debts and liabilities of the church to himself. Christ took to himself the punishment due to his people for their sins and he nailed them to the cross. He died taking the penalty for the sin of the elect. Thus, sinners are saved by works—by the works of Jesus Christ!

Christ's work on the cross has wonderful consequences for the ones who are recipients of it. First, it stays God's wrath and anger from coming on people (called *propitiation*). Deserved divine condemnation is thus taken care of. Christ became a curse for his people (Gal. 3:13). Second, believers' sins are covered by the work of Christ (called *expiation*). As Macleod says, 'Our disobedience is completely covered by the obedience of the Son of God' (*A Faith to Live By*, 135). Third, the work of Christ makes the elect people right with God (called *reconciliation*). All that Christ did on the cross brings peace between God and his people. No longer is there condemnation for them; forgiveness, harmony, and healing have been secured. As Paul says in Romans 8:1, 'There is therefore now no condemnation for those who are in Christ Jesus.'

Redemption is the work of God. He purchased his people with his own blood (Acts 20:28). In his letter to the Ephesians Paul points out that 'In him we have redemption through his blood, the forgiveness of our trespasses, according to the riches of his grace, which he lavished upon us' (1:7). Saved by works! Saved by works! Saved by the works of Jesus Christ!

The believer does not suffer eternally because of the suffering of Jesus Christ. On the cross he suffered the pain of the body, the pain of death, the pain in his soul, and the pain from heaven, earth, and hell. There he paid the wages of sin and condemnation. Isn't this a marvellous message? He suffered so that his people would be delivered from suffering. This is the gospel message about Jesus Christ and his awesome work on the cross. If you do not know him, will you turn to him this very hour?

Part IV:

Attitudes in Suffering: Encouragement for Believers

But resist him, firm in your faith, knowing that the same experiences of suffering are being accomplished by your brethren who are in the world. And after you have suffered for a little while, the God of all grace, who called you to His eternal glory in Christ will Himself perfect, confirm, strengthen and establish you. To Him be dominion forever and ever. Amen.

(1 Pet. 5:9-11)

When Mr. Bradford was told that his chain was a-buying, and that he must be burnt, he lifted up his eyes to heaven and said, 'I thank God for it; I have looked for this a long time; it comes not to me suddenly, but as a thing waited for every day, yea, every hour in the day; the Lord make me worthy thereof.' If upon God's warning you will but prepare for sufferings, you will never fear nor faint under sufferings, yea, then you will be able under the greatest persecutions to bear up bravely, and with holy Bradford bless the Lord that has called you to so high an honour as to count you worthy to suffer for his name.

(Thomas Brooks, *The Crown and Glory of Christianity*)

9

THE CROSS COMES BEFORE THE CROWN

It is a true statement of the divines that not only does the Christian taste the same afflictions as the unbeliever (albeit for different reasons), but no one on earth is exposed to suffering as the one seeking to live a godly life. Simply put, Christians ought to expect to suffer more than the world does. It appears as it should not be that way: the health/wealth proselytizers repeatedly assert that Christians should not suffer and the reason they do is because of a lack of faith. How frequently we hear that Christianity will do away with all your troubles on earth! One evangelist builds his entire message on the point that Christianity is one great party! How unthinkable! How absurd! Nowhere do the Scriptures promise that all believers will have no trials, persecutions, and sufferings—no, not once, never, not ever. On the contrary, God's Word tells us that those who desire to live a godly life in Christ Jesus will be a target of afflictions and will suffer more greatly than most people.

In the Bible, severe suffering is the *modus vivendi* of the people. Consider the lot of the Hebrews in Egypt: 'and [the Egyptians] made their lives bitter with hard labor in mortar and bricks and at all kinds of labor in the field, all their labors which they rigorously imposed on them' (Exod. 1:14). Certainly many died at the command of Pharaoh to cast the Hebrew children into the Nile River (Exod. 1:22). David, the man after God's own heart, was persecuted at the hands of many enemies, which included his son Absalom (2 Sam. 15, Ps. 3) and King Saul (1 Sam. 18ff.). Daniel was hurled into a den of lions because of his faith. Meshach, Shadrach, and Abed-nego endured the heat of the fiery furnace on account of holiness. The list of suffering believers could go on and on. The writer to the Hebrews expressed it this way when speaking of the godly of the Bible: 'They were stoned, they were sawn in two, they were tempted, they were put to death with the sword; they went about in sheepskins, in goatskins, being destitute, ill-treated (men of whom the world was not worthy), wandering in deserts and mountains and caves and holes in the ground' (Heb. 11:37-38). Such is the allotment of the people of God in Scripture!

In the history of the church in all ages, suffering has been the common experience and portion of God's people. John Foxe opens his famous *Book of Martyrs* by saying, 'The history of the church may almost be said to be a history of the trials and sufferings of its members, as experienced at the hands of wicked men.' It may rightfully be said that the foundation of the church is the blood of its martyrs. Foxe's book recounts the history of that persecution, beginning with the ten Roman persecutions (AD 67–303) and it ends with detailed descriptions of the numerous English martyrs of Foxe's own time (sixteenth century). Foxe tells of John Hooper who was condemned to death for his stance for biblical Christianity. Hooper was told he would be sent to Gloucester for execution, and he responded that he was delighted, praising God that he should be sent among the people to whom he had been pastor to confirm with his death the truth he had taught them. At his burning, Hooper spoke thus to the crowd:

> Lord, I am hell, but thou art heaven; I am swill and a sink of sin, but thou art a gracious God and a merciful Redeemer. Have mercy therefore upon me, most miserable and wretched offender, after thy great mercy, and according to thine inestimable goodness. Thou art ascended into heaven, receive me, hell, to be partaker of thy joys, where thou sittest in equal glory with thy Father. For well knowest thou, Lord, wherefore I am come hither to suffer, and why the wicked do persecute this thy poor servant; not for my sins and transgressions committed against them, but because I will not allow their wicked doings, to the contaminating of thy blood, and to the denial of the knowledge of thy truth, wherewith it did please thee, by thy Holy Spirit, to instruct me; the which, with as much diligence as a poor wretch might (being thereto called), I have set forth thy glory. And well seest thou, my Lord and God, what terrible pains and cruel torments be prepared for thy creature: such, Lord, as without thy strength none is able to bear, or patiently to pass. But all things that are impossible to man are possible with thee: therefore strengthen me of thy goodness, that in the fire I break not the rules of patience; or else assuage the terror of the pains, as shall seem most to thy glory.

Hooper was executed at the stake on February 9, 1555. Foxe describes the martyrdoms of many others who held to holiness, men such as Bradford, Latimer, Taylor, Cranmer, and Ridley. How many thousands of believers have been summoned to present the ultimate sacrifice! How many went joyfully to the stake or gallows for the sake of holiness, for the honor of Christ!

Some might argue that is no concern of us today because martyrdom is a thing of the past. Our present societies are so civilized that it would be unthinkable for such persecutions and sufferings to occur against the church. Let us not be so naive. By some estimates there have been more martyrs in the twentieth century than in any previous century. Consider the Boxer Rebellion in China at the turn of the century in which thousands of Christians, missionaries and citizens alike, were killed, imprisoned, or otherwise persecuted solely for their faith in the Deity. Since World War II, persecution appears to have escalated around the globe, most notably in the Soviet Union and the People's Republic of China. Untold numbers of believers were tortured, many unto death, in Idi Amin's Uganda, in Chile, in Kenya, in the Congo, and elsewhere. The Church has absolutely no reason to feel safe and comfortable in the world because the tenacious sceptre of martyrdom will continue to rear its ugly head. In reality, Christians ought to anticipate it. The world and the true Church are at odds and will never mix. The Apostle John expresses that point simply: 'Do not marvel, brethren, if the world hates you' (1 John 3:13).

Christians today should not be caught off guard when persecution storms upon them. In reality, it should be expected. The Apostle Peter exclaims, 'Beloved, do not be surprised at the fiery ordeal among you, which comes upon you for testing, as though some strange thing were happening to you' (1 Pet. 4:12). Do not be surprised! We should not be unaware because Jesus said it would be so. In John 15:20, he says, 'Remember the word that I said to you…' And in 21:12, 16-17, 'But before all these things, they will lay their hands on you and will persecute you … you will be delivered up even to parents and brothers and relatives and friends, and they will put some of you to death, and you will be hated by all on account of My name.' Again Jesus explains, 'These things I have spoken to you that in Me you have peace. In the world you have tribulation, but take courage; I have overcome the world' (John 16:33). The truth of the matter is believers should not be astonished when persecutions and afflictions overtake them. The cross comes before the crown. As the wilderness came before the land flowing with milk and honey, the crucifixion before the resurrection, so shall the way to heaven be covered with thorns of tribulation!

It is required to suffer and bear one's own cross for the sake of Christ. Jesus speaks of this duty when he says, 'If anyone wishes to come after Me, let him deny himself, and take up his cross daily, and follow Me' (Luke 9:23). And, again, the words of Jesus: 'Whoever does not carry his own cross and come after Me cannot be My disciple' (Luke 14:27). There is no easy way into the gates of heaven! The path is not strewn with riches, comfort, and glory. One cannot travel the road of Vanity Fair, visit all the sites, inhale deeply, indulge in its pleasures, and then expect to sail smoothly to the celestial city. Paul says, 'And indeed, all who desire to live godly in Christ Jesus will be persecuted' (2 Tim. 3:12). If a person is not undergoing trials, afflictions, and persecutions in this life then one ought to question his walk here on earth—godly or not? In the Book of Acts, Luke puts it this way: 'Through many tribulations we must enter the kingdom of God' (Acts 14:22).

Now most Christians will not have the privilege of suffering the maximum sacrifice of martyrdom for the sake of Jesus. However, that should make believers no less willing and desirous participants. The attitude of Christians should be readiness for such a clarion call from the Master. Consider the words of Paul to his friends at Caesearea just prior to his arrest in Jerusalem: 'What are you doing, weeping and breaking my heart? For I am ready not only to be bound, but even to die at Jerusalem for the name of the Lord Jesus' (Acts 21:13). We must act like Paul. We must gird up our loins like men (Job 38:3; Jer. 1:17), put on the full armour of God (Eph 6:11), be strong and courageous (Josh. 1:6), and actively seek to enter the fray of spiritual warfare. It may or may not cost us our lives, but that does not matter: we must live knowing that Christ may ask us to lay down our lives for his name's sake. Christians must be prepared to die at the hands of the wicked and to do so willingly and cheerfully.

Although it appears that only a portion of believers will be called to the extremity of martyrdom, all Christians suffer to one degree or another in this life. No believers are immune to affliction. If one is attempting to live for Christ, then persecutions naturally arise from the wicked. Most often they will come through verbal attack, but sometimes will reach the point of physical violence. In addition, we are all exposed to natural sufferings, such as pain, disease, and death. Tornadoes, hurricanes, and the like strike Christians. In this latter sense, we suffer in the same manner as the unbeliever. Jesus said, 'for He causes His sun to rise on the evil and the good, and sends rain on the righteous and the unrighteous' (Matt. 5:45).

But unlike the unbeliever, no matter how severe the affliction, there is one thing the Christian can count on: suffering will never destroy the Christian. They cannot and will not claim victory over the believer. Listen to the Apostle Paul writing to the Romans:

> Who shall separate us from the love of Christ? Shall tribulation, or distress, or persecution, or famine, or nakedness, or peril, or sword? Just as it is written, 'For Thy sake we are being put to death all day long; we were considered as sheep to be slaughtered.' But in all these things we overwhelmingly conquer

through Him who loved us. For I am convinced that neither death, nor life, nor angels, nor principalities, nor things present, nor things to come, nor powers, nor height, nor depth, nor any other created thing, shall be able to separate us from the love of God, which is in Christ Jesus our Lord.

(Rom. 8:35-9)

The state of the believer is truly characterized by the event of the burning bush at Horeb. That theophany symbolized the condition of the people of God in the flaming furnace of Egypt (Deut 4:20). And although Israel was under great affliction and oppression, she was not consumed much in the same way that the bush remained intact. And so the Christian may be beset by fiery trials, yet these fiery trials shall never, 'nay never', harm or destroy the child of God. Christians are like Meshach, Shadrach, and Abed-nego: Nebuchadnezzar had them thrown into a blazing furnace that had been heated seven times greater than normal. But those godly men were not incinerated or in any way consumed by the oppressive heat, smoke, and flames—in fact, not even were their clothes affected or their hair singed (Dan. 3:27). Daniel was cast into the lions' den, a trial indeed! But the ravenous animals could not destroy the man of God or harm him at all because God protected Daniel by locking the mouths of the beasts (Dan. 6:22). Paul was repeatedly severely attacked for his faith, as he says in 2 Corinthians 11:23-27:

Are they servants of Christ? (I speak as if insane) I more so, in far more imprisonments, beaten times without number, often in danger of death. Five times I received from the Jews thirty-nine lashes. Three times I was beaten with rods, once I was stoned, three times I was shipwrecked, a night and a day I have spent in the deep. I have been on frequent journeys, in dangers from rivers, dangers from robbers, dangers from my countrymen, dangers from the Gentiles, dangers in the city, dangers in the wilderness, dangers on the sea, dangers among false brethren; I have been in labor and hardship, through many sleepless nights, in hunger and thirst, often without food, in cold and exposure.

But even in the midst of such extreme sufferings Paul could declare, 'we are afflicted in every way, but not crushed; perplexed, but not despairing; persecuted, but not forsaken; struck down, but not destroyed; always carrying about in the body the dying Jesus, that the life of Jesus also may be manifested in our body' (2 Cor. 4:8-10).

The believer's great example of ultimate victory even through present, earthly suffering is Christ Jesus. What a life he lived, what a death he experienced. No one ever bore the sorrows or afflictions of our Lord. All the powers of evil and darkness surrounded him, beset him, and attacked him. He carried the sins, guilt, and debt of his people on his shoulders and nailed them to the cross. But was he destroyed? Defeated? Consumed? Never, never, never! For God 'raised Him from the dead, and seated Him at His right hand in the heavenly places, far above all rule and authority and power and dominion, and every name that is named, not only in this age, but also in the one to come' (Eph. 1:20-21). Christ lives and reigns this very day! What great encouragement that is to the believer who suffers: God will never abandon us nor forsake us. As Jesus, we will never be defeated in the end. Paul says, 'Now God has not only raised the Lord but will also raise us up through His power' (1 Cor. 6:14). We will be more than conquerors through him who loves us!

The sufferings of the reprobate serve a different purpose. They are merely a foretaste of the final end and fate of the ungodly. Yes, the unbeliever suffers here on earth, but it is nothing, a mere sip, in comparison to what he faces in the ages to come. Jesus spoke of the future of the wicked when he comes again this way: 'The Son of Man will send forth His angels, and they will gather out of His kingdom all stumbling blocks, and those who commit lawlessness, and will cast them into the furnace of fire; in that place where there shall be weeping and gnashing of teeth' (Matt. 13:41-42). Observe that the wicked are thrown into a fiery furnace as were the righteous, but for the ungodly there is no relief and no divine protection. It is like the guards of Nebuchadnezzar who were slain by the fire when they carried Shadrach, Meshach, and Abed-nego to the opening of the furnace (Dan. 3:22). Also, whereas Daniel was protected from the jaws of the lions, the ungodly who had maliciously attacked Daniel were thrown in ' … and they had not reached the bottom of the den before the lions overpowered them and crushed all their bones' (Dan. 6:24). Even such a pain of death for the unbeliever, however, is nothing compared to the eternal punishment and affliction that awaits them for eternity. Paul summarizes this contrast between the godly and the ungodly in the following manner: 'For the sorrow that is according to the will of God produces a repentance without regret, leading to salvation; but the sorrow of the world produces death' (2 Cor. 7:10).

It should be further noted that not only are believers strengthened through affliction but they flourish in it. Rather than diminish Christians and Christianity, suffering causes them to increase and abound. 'Grace grows best in winter' (S. Rutherford). When Pharaoh and the Egyptians attempted to destroy Israel in Exodus chapter 1, the text tells us: 'But the more they afflicted them, the more they multiplied and the more they spread out, so that they were in dread of the sons of Israel' (v. 12). John Foxe describes the first great Roman persecution of Christianity under Nero (c. AD 67) in the following manner:

> This was the occasion of the first persecution; and the barbarities exercised on the Christians were such as even excited the commiseration of the Romans themselves. Nero even refined upon cruelty, and contrived all manner of punishments for the Christians that the most infernal imagination could design. In particular, he had some sewed up in the skins of wild beasts, and then worried by dogs till they expired; and others dressed in shirts made stiff with wax, fixed to axletrees, and set on fire in his gardens, in order to illuminate them. This persecution was general throughout the whole Roman empire; *but it rather increased than diminished the spirit of Christianity* (emphasis added).

Times of affliction are when Christianity spreads the most, and when the Christian is strongest in his faith and walk with the Lord. *Sub pondere crescit*—being pressed, it grows. Christianity's greatest growth is when it is persecuted: the blood of the martyrs is the seed of the Church (M. Henry).

The Christian should also be encouraged in times of suffering because God will bear up his people no matter how precarious the situation. The Red Sea event in the Book of Exodus is a good example. God placed Israel in a seemingly impossible situation: the sea was at her back and the grand Egyptian army was marching at her front. What a trying circumstance for the people of God! What was Israel to do? They could not fight with any hope of victory, and they could not swim with any hope of deliverance. Hopeless, hopeless! But the God of salvation bore them on wings of eagles, redeemed them, and brought them to the land of promise. When in a dark hour, David was able to proclaim: 'The righteous cry and the LORD hears, and delivers them out of all their troubles

... Many are the afflictions of the righteous; but the LORD delivers him out of them all' (Ps. 34:17, 19). The psalmist again declares with great surety, 'Thou, who hast shown me many troubles and distresses, wilt revive me again, and wilt bring me up again from the depths of the earth' (Ps. 71:20). Toward the end of his life the Apostle Paul was able to write to his disciple Timothy: '... persecutions and sufferings, such as happened to me at Antioch, at Iconium and at Lystra; what persecutions I endured, and out of them all the Lord delivered me!' (2 Tim. 3:11). All Christians can take great comfort in the truth that no trials or tribulations will conquer them. God will simply not allow troubles to gain victory over the elect.

Yet, this does not mean that Christians will not be exposed to pain and suffering. All Christians suffer. All Christians lose loved ones. All Christians get sick. All Christians die. But even the severity of death will not defeat believers because God upholds them even in that extremity. At the conclusion of John Bunyan's allegory *Pilgrim's Progress*, the two characters, Christian and Hopeful, are about to cross the river of death in order to enter the gates of the celestial city (heaven). Bunyan relates the episode as follows:

> They then addressed themselves to the water; and entering, Christian began to sink, and crying out to his good friend Hopeful, he said, I sink in deep waters; the billows go over my head, all his waves go over me! Selah. Then said the other, Be of good cheer, my brother, I feel the bottom, and it is good. Then said Christian, Ah! I shall not see the land that flows with milk and honey; and with that a great darkness and horror fell upon Christian, so that he could not see before him. Also here he in great measure lost his senses, so that he could neither remember nor orderly talk of any of those sweet refreshments that he had met with in the way of his pilgrimage. But all the words that he spake still tended to discover that he had horror

of mind, and heart fears that he should die in that river, and never obtain entrance in at the gate. Here also, as they that stood by perceived, he was much in the troublesome thoughts of the sins that he had committed, both since and before he began to be a pilgrim. It was also observed that he was troubled with apparitions of hobgoblins and evil spirits, for ever and anon he would intimate so much by words.

Hopeful, therefore, here had much ado to keep his brother's head above the water; yea, sometimes he would be quite gone down, and then, ere a while, he would rise up again half dead. Hopeful also would endeavor to comfort him, saying, Brother, I see the gate, and men standing by to receive us: but Christian would answer, It is you, it is you they wait for; you have been hopeful ever since I knew you. And so have you, said he to Christian. Ah! brother! said he, surely if I was right he would now arise to help me: but for my sins he hath brought me into the snare, and hath left me. Then said Hopeful, My brother, you have quite forgot the text, where it is said of the wicked, *There are no bands in their death, but their strength is firm. They are not in trouble as other men, neither are they plagued like other men.* These troubles and distresses that you go through in these waters are no sign that God hath forsaken you; but are sent to try you, whether you will call to mind that which heretofore you have received of his goodness, and live upon him in your distresses.

Then I saw in my dream (says Bunyan), that Christian was as in a muse a while. To whom also Hopeful added this word, Be of good cheer, Jesus Christ maketh thee whole; and with that Christian brake out with a loud voice, Oh, I see him again! and he tells me, *When thou passest through the waters, I will be with thee and through the rivers, they shall not overflow thee.*

Jesus has conquered death and he has broken the chains of hell for the believer. We are more than conquerors through him who loved us! We may cry out with Paul: 'Death is swallowed up in victory. O Death, where is your victory? O Death, where is your sting?' (1 Cor. 15:54-55).

In his *A Faithful Narrative of Surprising Conversions*, Jonathan Edwards tells of a young woman who was converted after having lived a riotous life. But soon after her conversion she was beset by severe physical trials that ended in a slow, painful death. As she faced the dark, fearful unknown her faith was strengthened by the Lord to the point of joy and exultation. Edwards writes:

> She had great longings to die, that she might be with Christ; which increased till she thought she did not know how to be patient and wait till God's time should come … 'I am quite willing to live, and quite willing to die; quite willing to be sick, and quite willing to be well; and quite willing for anything that God will bring upon me! And then,' said she, 'I felt myself perfectly easy, in a full submission to the will of God' … The same week that she died, when she was in distressing circumstances as to her body, some of the neighbors who came to see her, asked if she was willing to die? She replied, that she was quite willing either to live or die; she was willing to be in pain; she was willing to be so always as she was then, if that was the will of God. She willed what God willed. They asked her whether she was willing to die that night? She answered, 'Yes, if it be God's will.' And seemed to speak all with that perfect composure of spirit, and with such a cheerful countenance, that it filled them with admiration.

Believers may rest assured that God will not abandon them at death. In an evil hour, David was able to proclaim, 'Even though I walk through the valley of the shadow of death, I fear no evil; for Thou art with me' (Ps. 23:4).

> Jesus! What a help in sorrow!
>   While the billows o'er me roll,
> even when my heart is breaking,
>   he, my comfort, helps my soul.

Hallelujah! What a Savior!
  Hallelujah! What a Friend!
Saving, helping, keeping, loving,
  he is with me to the end.

(J. Wilbur Chapman, 1910)

Another reason why suffering, even unto death, should not surprise Christians is because the earth is not our home. It is hostile territory. The Apostle Peter claims that we are nothing more than 'aliens and strangers' in the world (1 Pet. 2:11). We are not to love the world, but rather we are to follow in the footsteps of the Biblical saints who 'died in faith, without receiving the promises, but having seen them and having welcomed them from a distance, and having confessed that they were strangers and exiles on the earth' (Heb. 11:13). We simply do not belong here, but as Paul says, 'our citizenship is in heaven' (Phil. 3:20). Believers must be willing to let go of the flesh. Do not be like Lot's wife! She looked back because she could not let go of earthly things. Flee and gaze upon heavenly things! 'For here we do not have a lasting city, but we are seeking the city which is to come' (Heb. 13:14).

Great are the rewards for those who persevere for the sake of righteousness. Yes, the cross comes before the crown, but the crown does come! In reality, believers may reap some of those benefits in their earthly existence. For example, how you bear up in suffering may serve as evidence for others who watch you. Christians may be strengthened by your example and encouraged to fight the good fight. The Apostle Paul recognized that benefit from his own suffering, as he writes to the Corinthian Church: 'But if we are afflicted it is for your comfort and salvation; or if we are comforted, it is for your comfort, which is effective in the patient enduring of the same sufferings which we also suffer; and our hope for you is firmly grounded, knowing that as you are sharers of our sufferings, so also you are sharers of our comfort' (2 Cor. 1:6-7). A Christian's endurance in suffering may also prompt an unbeliever to reconsider his own condition and place in the scope of reality. Paul and Silas' patience in the midst of the great trial at Philippi resulted in the conversion of the jailer. Consequently, God may use our sufferings as a witness and an impulse to the non-Christian to turn from his wicked ways unto the only true God. Our hurt may be a prod for the salvation of another.

How the Christian endures affliction is present proof of an upright, godly character. In other words, the way a Christian faces pain and suffering serves as concrete evidence of a regenerate heart and of ongoing sanctification. Peter says as much to the early church that was in the midst of great persecution: 'In this you greatly rejoice, even though now for a little while, if necessary, you have been distressed by various trials, that *the proof of your faith*, being more precious than gold which is perishable, even though tested by fire, may be found to result in praise and glory and honor at the revelation of Jesus Christ' (1 Pet. 1:6-7). So, Christian, take courage in your suffering. Your perseverance is evidence of God's grace to you and of your faith in Him.

Through afflictions the Christian is also united here on earth with other Christians who are exposed to suffering. In *Pilgrim's Progress*, Bunyan pictures Christian entering the Valley of the Shadow of Death (symbolic of great trials), and he comments:

The pathway was here also exceedingly narrow, and therefore good Christian was the more put to it; for when he sought, in the dark, to shun the ditch on the one hand, he was ready to tip over the mire on the other; also when he sought to escape the mire, without great carefulness he would be ready to fall into the ditch. Thus he went on, and I heard him here sigh bitterly; for, besides the dangers mentioned above, the pathway was here so dark, and ofttimes, when he lift his foot to set forward, he knew not where or upon what he should set it next … About the midst of the valley, I perceived the mouth of hell to be, and it stood also hard by the wayside. Now, thought Christian, what shall I do?

Christian is comforted, however, because:

he thought he heard the voice of a man, as going before him, saying, Though I walk through the valley of the shadow of death, I will fear no evil, for thou art with me. Then he was glad … because he gathered from thence, that some who feared God were in this valley as well as himself.

As Christians, we do not walk the path of suffering alone. We do not die alone. Not only has Jesus gone on before, but other Christians are travelling right beside us. When Latimer and Ridley were martyred at the stake together because of their stand for holiness, Latimer encouraged his friend: 'Be of good comfort, master Ridley, and play the man. We shall this day light such a candle, by God's grace, in England, as I trust shall never be put out.' What courage! What comfort! As Peter teaches, 'resist him, firm in your faith, knowing that the same experiences of suffering are being accomplished by your brethren who are in the world' (1 Pet. 5:9).

In addition, on the road of affliction the Christian is united with the martyred saints of history. We are joined with men such as Noah, Abraham, Moses and others (Heb. 11) who 'died in faith, without receiving the promises' (v. 13). The author to the Hebrews emphasizes this point when he says, 'And all these men having gained approval through their faith, did not receive what was promised, because God had provided something better for us, *so that apart from us they should not be made perfect*' (italics added) (Heb. 11:39-40). Believers are, therefore, one community of faith and suffering throughout history, a continuum beginning with Adam and extending even unto today. The Biblical writer comments on the major consequence of that continuity: 'Therefore, since we have so great a cloud of witnesses surrounding us, let us lay aside every encumbrance, and the sin which so easily entangles us, and let us run with endurance the race that is set before us, fixing our eyes on Jesus, the author and perfecter of faith, who for the joy set before Him endured the cross, despising the shame, and has sat down at the right hand of the throne of God' (Heb. 12:1-2).

Suffering also advances our rewards in heaven. As the Apostle Paul teaches, believers are 'heirs of God and fellow heirs with Christ, if indeed we suffer with Him in order that we may also be glorified with Him. For I consider that the sufferings of this present time are not worthy to be compared with the glory that is to be revealed to us' (Rom. 8:17-18). And he says elsewhere, 'For momentary, light affliction is producing for us an eternal weight of glory far beyond all comparison...' (2 Cor. 4:17). And we have this promise from the Apostle Peter:'And after you have suffered for a little while, the God of all grace, who called you to His eternal glory in Christ will Himself perfect, confirm, strengthen and establish you' (1 Pet. 5:10). Indeed, the celestial city with all its beauty, glory, and benefits awaits the Christian who perseveres unto the end. At the end of Christian's journey in *Pilgrim's Progress* Bunyan describes the scene of Christian and Hopeful being welcomed into the heavenly city:

Now I saw in my dream that these two men went in at the gate: and lo, as they entered, they were transfigured, and they had raiment put on that shone like gold. There was also those that met them with harps and crowns, and gave to them—the harps to praise withal, and the crowns in token of honour. Then I heard in my dream that all the bells in the city rang again for joy, and that it was said unto them, Enter ye into the joy of your Lord. I also heard the men themselves, that they sang with a loud voice, saying, Blessing and honour, and glory, and power, be unto him that sitteth upon the throne, and unto the Lamb, for ever and ever.

Present pain and suffering are nothing compared to the glory that Christ has bought and secured for us in heaven. So, Christian, be encouraged in your earthly trials, for 'It is trustworthy statement: for if we died with Him, we shall also live with Him; if we endure, we shall also reign with Him' (2 Tim. 2:11-12); and, again, 'Blessed is a man who perseveres under trial; for once he has been approved, he will receive the crown of life, which the Lord has promised to those who love Him' (James 1:12).

Finally, the Scriptures not only call us to be patient with and to endure suffering, but they also demand that we do it joyfully. How often the apostles combine the concepts of suffering and joy! James says, 'Consider it all joy, my brethren, when you encounter various trials' (James 1:2). Paul also comments, 'And not only this, but we also exult in our tribulations, knowing that tribulation brings about perseverance...' (Rom. 5:3); again, 'I rejoice in my sufferings' (Col 1:24); and, we are 'sorrowful yet always rejoicing' (2 Cor. 6:10).

Dear Christian, my prayer is that you would bear up under your trials—no matter what they be, even unto death—with great patience, hope and joy. May we glorify God who strengthens us to endure. May we remember that we have a Saviour who has travelled this path of misery and will never allow us to be snatched out of his hand: 'For you have been called for this purpose (to suffer), since Christ also suffered for you, leaving you an example for you to follow in His steps' (1 Pet. 2:21). In the steps of Jesus! Lord, make us worthy to travel that path!

If nothing else will do to sever me from my sins, Lord, send me such sore and trying calamities as shall awake me from earthly slumbers. It must always be best to be alive to Thee, whatever be the quickening instrument. I tremble as I write, for Oh! on every hand do I see too likely occasions for sore afflictions.

(Robert Murray McCheyne, November 21, 1832)

And as he passed by, he saw a man blind from birth. And his disciples asked him, saying, 'Rabbi, who sinned, this man or his parents, that he should be born blind?' Jesus answered, 'It was neither that this man sinned, nor his parents; but it was in order that the works of God might be displayed in him.'

(John 9:1-3)

10

Conclusion:
A Question of Prosperity

We have spent much of this book discussing why people, both believers and unbelievers, suffer. We now want to turn for a few pages to discuss the opposite problem, but as one will soon see it is a companion to the first nine chapters of the book. It is the question of prosperity. And this issue I have found to be quite troubling for the Christian. Let us state it directly: why do the wicked prosper? Why do people who do not know the Lord, who often devise vain things, who often set traps and snares for believers—why are they often successful in this life? Why is it that men who are immoral become some of the political leaders of our nations? Why do the most profane individuals gain the greatest wealth? Again, this is a troubling and vexing issue for many Christians. And it is particularly burdensome for the believer who understands that God is sovereign, and nothing happens in heaven or on earth apart from his will. There is the rub—if God is in control of all things, how could such injustice, as the wicked prospering, exist on earth?

Psalm 73 provides us with the answers, the divine answers, to these many troubling questions. We want to turn to that passage, and uncover its teachings. So, pay heed, dear Christian, and take note of what the psalmist tells us for our edification and understanding.

1 Surely God is good to Israel, to those who are pure in heart!
This is the foundational tenet and teaching of Psalm 73. God cares for his people, he loves his people, and the things he gives to them are for their good and benefit. As Paul says, 'And we know that God causes all things to work together for good to those who love God, to those who are called according to his purpose' (Rom. 8:28). Note Paul's emphasis on 'all things'; this is an acknowledgment of the sovereignty and providence of God. No matter what happens to us, God is bringing it upon us for our good.

No doubt, many of us would agree that God is good to his people. We would give a resounding 'amen' to that statement. Yet, I wonder how deeply embedded that truth is in our hearts. We often parrot the doctrines of sovereignty, providence, and grace, but do we live as if these things are true? Do these grand doctrines merely reside in our minds, as an intellectual truth, but not deep in our hearts?

2 But as for me, my feet came close to stumbling; my steps had almost slipped.
Are we not like the psalmist in this verse? We proclaim the truth of verse 1, but something happens to cause us to retreat from it. We surrender to apparent injustice, and we give up on the sovereignty of God. What is it that would have such a seditious, undercutting effect?

3 For I was envious of the arrogant, as I saw the prosperity of the wicked.
Why is the psalmist jealous of the unrighteous? It is because
they are recipients of prosperity. The term in Hebrew for
'prosperity' is related to the word 'shalom'—it means to have
harmony, fulfilment, and completeness. And it is true that when
one looks at many unbelievers it appears that they are living
fulfilled, satisfied lives. From a human perspective, it appears
that God is good to the unbeliever, and often it seems that he is
better to them than to the Christian! This really seems unjust;
how could God be sovereign over that inequality?

*4-5 For there are no pains in their death; and their body is fat. They
are not in trouble as other men; nor are they plagued like mankind.*
The psalmist now employs hyperbole to demonstrate his
point. He looks at the death of the unbeliever, and really it is
no different than that of the believer. And sometimes they do
not have as many pains as the Christian in death. That does not
seem right! And besides that, the text literally says, that 'their
belly is fat.' That, of course, is a symbol of great prosperity and
wealth. Thus, when the psalmist makes a physical, by sight,
inspection of the unbeliever, all he sees is success. I have an
unbelieving friend from college who vowed that his goal in
life was to make a million dollars by the time he was 35 years
old—he succeeded. And a physical inspection of him would
say 'money'—he drives an expensive sports car and wears the
latest designer suits—he looks like prosperity.

In verse 5 the psalmist again employs hyperbole by saying
that unbelievers do not have the troubles of believers. At least
it often appears that way. The reality is that their troubles are
frequently no different than a believer's. How can that be in
a world run by a sovereign, just God?

6 Therefore pride is their necklace; the garment of violence covers them. The psalmist's displeasure and discouragement is further heightened by the unbeliever's attitude. Many of them are haughty, and full of pride because they believe they are the source of their own prosperity, as if it were their own doing. And their character is one of hostility and violence. 'Might is right' is their motto. And they wear these things like clothes for everyone to see. These are their glory and splendour, the things that they relish. And they want to show them off.

7 Their eye bulges from fatness; the imaginations of their heart run riot. What a vivid figure of speech! By reason of pampering and gluttony, even the eyes of the wicked are fat. What a sense of unmitigated, boundless greed. Calvin said of these people, 'They so glut and intoxicate themselves with their prosperity, that afterwards they are ready to burst…' Their arrogance and pride simply overflow.

8-9 They mock and wickedly speak of oppression; they speak from on high. They have set their mouth against the heavens, and their tongue parades through the earth.
The prosperity of the wicked results in their verbal gloating. They mock the righteous, speak evil things, and oppress others. They are insolent and speak to frighten and intimidate others. And they do this from self-elevated places. They make themselves out to be 'a distinct class of beings' (Calvin) above all other people. In fact, verse 9 literally says, 'they set their mouth in the heavens,' as if they are gods speaking forth divine speech.

There is nothing to stop their vainglorious and presumptive speech, to the point that 'their tongue parades through the earth.' This is another astute picture presented by the psalmist. The wicked's tongue parades through the earth: it receives all the accolades of mankind as it spews forth its unbounded and unbridled speech. Flattery, flattery, flattery!

16 When I pondered to understand this, it was troublesome in my sight. Here a few verses later the psalmist restates the problem: the prosperity of the wicked in light of a sovereign, loving God is troubling. So he ponders, reasons, and rationally tries to understand the issue. But even then it continues to be a snare.

17 Until I came into the sanctuary of God; then I perceived their end. The psalmist goes to worship in the temple with other believers. All the cares of the world are shunned and put aside. It is here that spiritual discernment and godly perception arrive. The answer to the problem is provided: it is 'their end.' The wicked appear to prosper now, but what ultimately happens to them? Where do they sit in the grand scheme of things? In the light of eternity, are they really prosperous? No. The success of the wicked is mere illusion; it is temporal and temporary; it is fleeting and short-lived! It is merely of this earth and a prosperity of sight only.

18 Surely thou dost set them in slippery places; thou dost cast them down to destruction.
The truth of the matter is set forth in this verse. Note how the psalmist begins by saying 'Surely'—this is the same term used in verse 1, in which he said that 'Surely God is good to Israel.' Thus, as certain and sure is the doctrine of God's goodness to Israel is the way in which he deals in judgement with unbelievers. God has truly set the wicked in slippery places in which they will easily fall. They think they are being prosperous by amassing possessions, gold and silver, and power, and fame, but it is these very things that God uses to topple them. Such

things provide no meaning, purpose, or significance—they are mere chaff that the wind quickly blows away. As Billy Graham used to say, 'One can not take the moving van to the cemetery.'

26 My flesh and my heart may fail, but God is the strength of my heart and my portion forever.

To the contrary, for the believer it is not health and wealth that give meaning and significance to life. Those things perish. But what ultimately matters, and lasts for eternity, is if one belongs to God or not. This is the only division of relevance in the human race. Such distinctions as rich/poor, slave/free, and black/white will not survive this life. But the distinction between the righteous man who loves Christ and his word and the unrighteous man who does not will last for eternity, as long as heaven and hell themselves.

In Ecclesiastes 6:1-12, Solomon deals with the same issue of the apparent inequity of why many wicked are wealthy and many righteous are poor. He claims that a wise evaluation of mankind's outward fortunes will truly help to explain the apparent unfairness of God's plan and sovereignty. Why are God's people not better off than those who do not belong to him?

In verses 1-7, Solomon provides three illustrations to demonstrate that prosperity is not always or necessarily good.

1-2 There is an evil which I have seen under the sun and it is prevalent among men—a man to whom God has given riches and wealth and honor so that his soul lacks nothing of all that he desires, but God has not empowered him to eat from them, for a foreigner enjoys them.

Here is a man with lots of money and material possessions. But 'God has not empowered him to eat from them.' This is a euphemism that means that God has not allowed the man to enjoy what he has been given. It was not in the plan of God for that man to take satisfaction in things. This is a man who has riches, but no grace to enjoy them.

He ought to be contrasted to the man of Ecclesiastes 5:19, which says, 'Furthermore, as for every man to whom God has given riches and wealth, he has also empowered him to eat from them and to receive his reward and rejoice in his labor; this is the gift of God.' That is one difference between the believer and the unbeliever: the believer has been empowered by God's grace to be in relationship with him and to see all things in perspective to him. The unbeliever has no such perspective, assurance, or comfort.

How many people do we know like this man? Those who have wealth and many material possessions but are very unhappy and broken. Consider a person like Howard Hughes who had every physical enjoyment imaginable, but he died a recluse with no happiness or claim to satisfaction. The irony is that it is these very things that the world tells us to pursue. The world tells us that these things can give us satisfaction, contentment, and happiness: the lie of the age.

The conclusion then is that the wealth of a wicked man is not a sign of blessedness. We should not be fooled regarding the true state of a man merely by viewing the outward appearance. And the opposite is also true: because a person does not have a lot of wealth or good health in no way reflects that he has not been blessed by God. Consider a person like J. Hudson Taylor, a man of little financial means, who went to live among the impoverished in China. Does his wealth, or lack thereof, truly reflect his standing before God, or his satisfaction, or contentment? Ecclesiastes in no way teaches a health/wealth gospel that says if you have enough faith God will bless you financially and physically. That is a fallacy of

21st century Christianity that is being propagated by many evangelists and many churches. Health and wealth are the ways in which humans judge God's blessings, but it is not necessarily God's own judgement.

3-5 If a man fathers a hundred children and lives many years, however many they be, but his soul is not satisfied with good things, and he does not even have a proper burial, then I say, 'Better the miscarriage than he, for it comes in futility and goes into obscurity; and its name is covered in obscurity. It never sees the sun and it never knows anything; it is better off than he.'

Solomon considers a second man who appears to have been greatly blessed and prosperous, but is, like the first man, probably ungodly. This man fathers a hundred children. In the ancient Near East, the number of children, especially males, was a desirable thing. The ancients believed that it demonstrated great blessings from God. He also lives a long time. Old age was something sought after in ancient times, and was seen as a sign of prosperity.

But there is a problem. The soul of this man 'is not satisfied with these good things.' The word for 'satisfied' normally means 'to be filled up with food.' This man has been given many things but his appetite for more is never quenched. How many people do we know like this, in which what they have is never enough?

Solomon's conclusion is clear: the idea that a wicked man has a large family and long life is not necessarily a sign of blessedness and true prosperity. We should not be fooled regarding the character and state of a man merely by outward appearance. The opposite is just as true. Just because a person has a short life and no family does not mean that he was not blessed. Consider the figure of Robert Murray McCheyne. He died at the age of 29, never having been married. But God greatly blessed him and his ministry. And that beyond many who have lived five score and beyond.

6-7 Even if the other man lives a thousand years twice and does not enjoy good things—do not all go to one place? All a man's labor is for his mouth and yet the appetite is not satisfied.

Solomon uses hyperbole to describe the third man. Here is a man who lives two thousand years. Isn't that a sign of blessing and prosperity? Talk about health! Yet, if he does not have a relationship with the Creator and be empowered with the ability to enjoy life, he will never be satisfied or content. Long life simply can not give meaning and purpose to life. So, in reality, a person may have riches, honor, longevity, and many children, and yet be a broken, unhappy, alone person. Things are not always what they seem to be. *Prosperity without the divine gift of enjoyment is vanity.* And so the wicked only seem or appear to prosper.

A companion truth to the one just mentioned is that suffering, adversity, and poverty are not necessarily signs of God's disfavour. In fact, Solomon argues that sometimes adversity is a greater good than prosperity. In 6:12, he asks the question, 'who knows what is good for a man during his lifetime?' Down through history, and clearly in our day, many answer by saying that material prosperity is the highest good for humanity. Who is it that our children emulate? Who are their models? Those who are rich and famous. How easily Christians fall into this: we look at someone who is wealthy and well-known, and we think that person has been exceedingly blessed by God. In Ecclesiastes 7, Solomon is going to turn this thought upside down. He claims that there are some things that are better than prosperity. In fact, sometimes adversity is better than prosperity.

1a A good name is better than a good ointment.

A good name, that is, that one is considered a noble, courageous person of upright character, is better than expensive perfume. A good reputation, then, is more abiding than material riches. So a man with integrity, although poor, has really been more blessed than the ungodly with storerooms full of treasures. Thus, when we consider the question 'what is good for a man' we ought to consider his character before his pocketbook. Who is the one truly prospering?

1b-4 And the day of one's death is better than the day of one's birth. It is better to go to a house of mourning than to go to a house of feasting, because that is the end of every man, and the living takes it to heart. Sorrow is better than laughter, for when a face is sad a heart may be happy. The mind of the wise is in the house of mourning, while the mind of fools is in the house of pleasure.

We have already dealt with these verses in chapter 6 of this book, and so we will say little here but to point the reader in that direction. The passage simply means that in times of sorrow and troubles, people are confronted with their condition on the earth. Times of laughter and feasting rarely have bring forth such issues. It is in difficult times that we learn something of ourselves, and obtain some knowledge of our hearts. That is good. We normally think that the one who is partying and in gaiety must be blessed by God, but that may not be true at all.

5-6 It is better to listen to the rebuke of a wise man than for one to listen to the song of fools. For as the crackling of thorn bushes under a pot, so is the laughter of the fool, and this too is futility.

What is good for a man? It is better to be chastised by a knowledgeable person that to be festive with the fool. But who wants to be chastised? Yet, on the other hand, we may learn something of ourselves and change our ways because of a wise rebuke. It might be good for us. The world tells us something different: laughter means pleasure and rebuke is bad. But that simply may not be true. Chastisement may bring about long-lasting, good results. Laughter of the fool, on the other hand, is like the burning of thorn bushes under a pot—it is quickly gone and short-lived.

7 For oppression makes a wise man mad, and a bribe corrupts the heart.
Integrity and honour are better than riches. Here is a man who is angry about oppression for monetary gain. Justice is a greater good than wealth. So, who has really been blessed by God? The man who is rich by taking advantage of others, or the poor man with integrity and honour?

8-9 The end of a matter is better than its beginning; patience of spirit is better than haughtiness of spirit. Do not be eager in your heart to be angry, for anger resides in the bosom of fools.
Patience is much better than pride. The one who takes the long view and is willing to wait for delayed gratification is better than one who demands immediate results, instant gratification. It goes without saying that our society increasingly has become one in which its members want immediate results, satisfaction, and fulfilment. We no longer have a sense that good things are worth waiting for.

Patience is much better than anger. It is a sign of wisdom, whereas anger symbolizes foolishness. Anger resides in the very hearts and bosoms of the fools; Christians are not to be like them.

10 Do not say, 'Why is it that the former days were better than these?' For it is not from wisdom that you ask about this.
One should not wish for days gone by with their real or imagined advantages and pleasures. Nostalgia can be fool's gold. Wise people understand that God has ordained all things and all times. Everything unfolds according to his sovereign plan. So today has been foreordained as was yesteryear, and we must accept it as we have accepted the past. In addition, wise people know that present trouble may be of greater benefit than past pleasures. Troubling things can hone our character and make us perseverant and strong.

11-12 Wisdom along with an inheritance is good and an advantage to those who see the sun. For wisdom is protection just as money is protection. But the advantage of knowledge is that wisdom preserves the lives of its possessors.

Wisdom is better than money. Solomon does not say that money is bad or evil, only that wisdom is better. There is nowhere in the whole section that he says that money is evil, for it is not. But he does emphasize that there are some things that have more value and are more advantageous for mankind. Wisdom is one of those things. It is good to be godly and to strive after the things of God.

13-14 Consider the work of God, for who is able to straighten what he has bent? In the day of prosperity be happy, but in the day of adversity consider—God has made the one as well as the other so that man may not discover anything that will be after him.

This is the climax of the section. The truth of the matter is that affliction and pleasure are both the appointments of God. After Job was afflicted, he turned to his wife and said, 'Shall we indeed accept good from God and not accept adversity?' (Job 2:10). Yes, in prosperous times we are to be happy and acknowledge the good gifts of God. In times of adversity, we need to recognize that he has brought those upon us also for our benefit.

It is at this point that we need to be careful. We often make premature and surface judgements regarding a man's situation and condition. We say that a man is blessed by God because he is wealthy, and cursed by God if he has adversity in life. This may simply not be true! We must penetrate more deeply to see and properly evaluate the plan of God.